Radical Left Parties

Yiannos Katsourides

Radical Left Parties in Government

The Cases of SYRIZA and AKEL

palgrave
macmillan

Yiannos Katsourides
Social and Political Sciences
University of Cyprus
Nicosia, Cyprus

ISBN 978-1-349-95465-0   ISBN 978-1-137-58841-8   (eBook)
DOI 10.1057/978-1-137-58841-8

Printed on acid-free paper

This Palgrave Macmillan imprint is published by Springer Nature
The registered company is Macmillan Publishers Ltd.

PREFACE

Debates about participating in state institutions and the government had been a matter of fiery contests among various Marxist and neo-Marxist movements, parties, and organizations not only in the late nineteenth and early twentieth centuries but also in the 1960s and 1970s. The resurface of the debate in the latter period was at the centre of western Marxism not without reason. During this period, several important events took place (see Chap. 2). The fall of the Union of Soviet Socialist Republics (USSR) in 1991, however, put these discussions and quests into the background for many years.

As often quoted although, history tends to repeat itself. Twenty years after capitalism and liberal democracy were thought to have won the battle in a definitive manner (Fukuyama 1992), this was again questioned. The reason for this was the new Great Recession that brought the issue of government participation onto the agenda of radical Left parties (RLPs). Many parties of this family emerged as serious or at least considerable government contenders and/or coalition partners all over Europe, including among others:

- In Greece the Coalition of the Radical Left (SYRIZA) rose to power within a time frame of three years
- In Cyprus the Progressive Party of the Working People (AKEL) had governed from 2008–2013
- In Portugal the Portugese Communist Party (PCP) and the Left Bloc (BE) were offering support to the Socialist government

- In Spain the Podemos' share of votes had risen to 20 % by the 2015 elections and proposed a coalition government with the socialists
- In France J.-L. Melenchon scored 11 % in the 2012 presidential elections
- In Germany the German Left Party (Die Linke) polled 8.6 % in the 2013 national elections coming in third

After years of political marginalization the radical Left seemed to have acquired political visibility once again.

The Greek anti-austerity, left-wing party, SYRIZA's recent electoral victory and rise to power in particular electrified the Left all over Europe. SYRIZA stormed to power after years of harsh austerity in the country and provided a model that was acceptable even for moderate social democrats who had struggled in search of ideas and inspiration since the onset of the economic crisis in 2008. Other parties of the (radical) Left took inspiration from this achievement. In discussions of SYRIZA's surprising victory, however, it is often forgotten that theirs was not the first victory of a RLP; in 2008 the Cypriot AKEL was elected to power in the Republic of Cyprus, holding the presidency until 2013.

Although these two parties come from very similar cultural settings (i.e., Greece and Cyprus share many common features) notwithstanding their significant differences, they have never been studied in comparison, only in isolation. This book's aim is to bring the experiences of the two parties together and place them in the context of RLPs' politics mostly with regard to the issue of government participation. Thus, the chapters illustrate and analyze how the two parties came to power and compare stheir governing styles, focusing especially on their ability to fulfil—with regard to their radical identity—their electoral promises once in office. Furthermore, the book addresses the circumstances of radical Left politics in two small countries on the European periphery, which some commentators view as exemplars of a much (needed) wider European change.

The book analyzes the trajectory of the two parties from opposition to governing, focusing on 'how' they came to power and how they behaved while in office. By examining these parties' trajectories, it is possible to put forward larger and more substantive questions that can go beyond their isolated experience in government. That is, questions that are related not only to the history and current trajectory of the RLP family but also with regard to the path of the European Union (EU) in contemporary times, amid a multifaceted crisis (i.e., economic, trust, legitimacy, etc.).

University of Cyprus   Yiannos Katsourides
Nicosia, Cyprus

ACKNOWLEDGMENTS

Although only my name appears on the cover of this book, there are a great many people who have contributed to its publication—some without even knowing it—and to whom I owe my thanks. Costas Gouliamos always has been there to listen and give advice. Michalis Spourdalakis's insightful comments at different stages of my research were thought-provoking and helped me focus my ideas. I am extremely thankful to Antonis Ellinas for encouraging me to write this book and for his constructive criticism and comments on an earlier version of the manuscript. I am grateful to the anonymous reviewers for his and her reviews and suggestions on the book proposal and the draft manuscript; these helped me expand and develop my ideas and approaches.

I am also indebted to Luke March, Costas Eleftheriou, Yiannakis Kolokasides, Michalis Michael, Andreas Panayiotou, Caesar Mavratsas, and my students; I had many valuable discussions about the book with all of those named here. I would like to acknowledge the work of Kathy Stephanides for language and copyediting of the entire book, as well as Imogen Gordon Clark, Ambra Finotello, and Jemina Warren at Palgrave Macmillan for their patience and guidance throughout the production and publishing process.

Portions of certain chapters draw on ideas originally presented in my articles 'Travelling against the Tide: The Cypriot Communist Left in the Post-1990 Era' and 'Organizational Continuity and Party Strength: The Communist Party of Cyprus' (co-authored with Antonis Ellinas); these were published, respectively, in *Perspectives on European Politics and Society* and *West European Politics*. The book makes use of a significant number of Greek sources intentionally in order to convey to a wider (English-speaking) audience the many analyses and opinions from within the two countries.

None of this would have been possible without the encouragement and patience of my family, and especially my wife Yiota, who has supported me throughout this endeavor. Still, there is one person who has my eternal gratitude and to whom I will always owe much more than I ever told her while she was alive. This is my late mother, Androula, to whom I dedicate this book.

Contents

LIST OF ABBREVIATIONS

17N	17 November (Greek Terrorist Group)
ADISOK	Renewed Democratic Socialist Movement (Cyprus)
AEKA	Renewing Modernizing Movement of the Left
AKEL	Progressive Party of the Working People (Cyprus)
ANEL	Independent Greeks Party
ANTARSYA	Anticapitalist Left Cooperation for the Overthrow (Greece)
ATTAC	Association for the Taxation of Financial Transactions and Citizen's Action
BE	Left Bloc (Portugal)
CPC	Communist Party of Cyprus
CTP	Republican Turkish Party (Cyprus)
Die Linke	The Left (Germany)
DIKO	Democratic Party (Cyprus)
DIMAR	Democratic Left (Greece)
DISY	Democratic Rally (Cyprus)
EAR	Greek Left
EC	European Commission
ECB	European Central Bank
EDA	United Democratic Left (Greece)
EDEK	United Democratic Union of the Centre (Cyprus)
EDH	United Democrats (Cyprus)
EDON	United Democratic Youth Organization (Cyprus)
EEC	European Economic Community
EKA	Union of Cypriot Farmers
EL	Party of the European Left
EL	Red-Green Alliance (Denmark)
EOKA	National Organization of Cypriot Fighters

EP	European Parliament
EPALXI	Front for the Restoration of the Center
EU	European Union
EEC	European Economic Community
FG	Left Front (France)
GAL	Green-Alternative-Libertarian
GUE/NGL	European United Left/Nordic Green Left
IMF	International Monetary Fund
KKE	Communist Party of Greece
KKE-*Es*	Communist Party of Greece (Interior)
KOE	(Maoist) Communist Organization of Greece
META	Militant Workers/Employees Class Overturning
NATO	North Atlantic Treaty Organization
ND	New Democracy (Greece)
NLL	Non Leftist Left
LAE	Popular Unity (Greece)
PASOK	Pan-Hellenic Socialist Movement (Greece)
PCE	Communist Party of Spain
PCF	Communist Party of France
PCI	Communist Party of Italy
PCP	Communist Party of Portugal
PEO	Pancyprian Federation of Labour
POGO	Pancyprian Federation of Women's Organization (Cyprus)
PSF	French Socialist Party
PSOE	Spanish Socialist Workers Party
RLPs	Radical Left parties
SP	Socialist Party (the Netherlands)
SYRIZA	Coalition of the Radical Left (Greece)
Synaspismos	Coalition of Left and Progress
TAN	Traditional-Authoritarian-Nationalist
TINA	There Is No Alternative
USSR	United Soviet Socialist Republics
WWII	World War II

LIST OF TABLES

CHAPTER 1

Introduction

Abstract This book focuses on radical Left parties in government and the impact of governing on their radical character. The introductory section considers, first, issues related to the conceptualization and definition of radical Left parties, one of the most important being the European integration project. Second, this chapter examines the contemporary social, economic, and political conditions that have led to the most recent Left governance in some countries. Two issues are highlighted: coercive Europeanization and austeritarianism. The third section presents this book's frame of analysis, which revolves around the vote-office-policy trichotomy of party goals. The final section explains the selection of case studies and the book's methodology.

Keywords Radical Left parties • European Union (EU) • Europeanization • Economic crisis • Austerity • Vote-office-policy • AKEL • SYRIZA • Greece • Cyprus

Substantial research on the status of the radical and communist Left parties was undertaken during the first years after the collapse of the Soviet bloc; however, interest in these parties soon faded, likely because of their minimal impact on national political systems. This earlier research—as well as even quite recent research—tended to focus on the Left's issues such as ideological identity, forms of organization, relationship to their past, and the organizational and ideological adaptation and/or transformation

© The Editor(s) (if applicable) and The Author(s) 2016
Y. Katsourides, *Radical Left Parties in Government*,
DOI 10.1057/978-1-137-58841-8_1

required to cope with the new environment, and so on (e.g., see March 2011; March and Mudde 2005; Dunphy 2004; Botella and Ramiro 2003; Bosco 2001; Boggs 1995; Bull and Heywood 1994; Bell 1993). There has been relatively little investigation into Left strategies targeting governance and how these might affect its radical identity (e.g., Dunphy and Bale 2011; Olsen et al. 2010; Dunphy 2007).

There are obvious reasons for the lack of research in this area: the radical/communist Left parties are most often very small and usually relatively insignificant, and most of them are unable, unwilling, or not sought after to form part of governing coalitions. That there is renewed interest, however, is not surprising given that the radical Left is increasingly a stabilized, consolidated, and permanent actor on the European political scene; as such it has become a principal challenger to mainstream social democratic parties (March 2012: 314) that seem to have run out of ideas (Moschonas 2010).

Nevertheless, the attitude of radical Left parties (hereafter RLPs) towards government participation is acknowledged as the biggest change in the radical Left's strategy since the Cold War (March 2008: 13). Between 1947 and 1989, in no country other than Finland, was the Communist party a regular participant in government; since 1989 there have been a number of coalition governments with Left party representation. By mid-2016 most RLPs (although not extreme Left parties) in fact no longer viewed bourgeois parliaments and social democratic parties as designed to deceive the working class. Radical Left parties have increasingly become open to forming coalition governments with social democrats and Greens, or at least willing to offer ad hoc cooperation in parliaments and support for social democrat minority governments (Daiber and Kulke 2010). This signals their transition from outsider to insider parties (Olsen et al. 2010: 2).

The previous debate over whether communist parties should pursue power in the national or the pan-European context is once again resurfacing, especially because of the convergence and interdependence of globalization and Europeanization and, most importantly, the recent economic crisis. Although many RLPs' goal is for government participation on a national level, they do so as part of a European Left strategy that aims for leftist parties to take the reins of their own governments so that they can effect or facilitate changes in the European Union (EU). However, today's radical Left milieu is complex and diverse, thus necessitating a minimum operationalization of this party family.

DEFINING THE RADICAL LEFT

Although the concept of party families has been a useful tool for the comparison and analysis of party systems in European democracies (Mair and Mudde 1998), it is not without problems, especially in the so-called post-ideological era (Elff 2013). This applies to all manner of party families, and the radical Left is no exception.

Historical legacies and diverse ideological outlooks add to the problems and particularly within the Left. In this regard, the Russian Revolution marked not only the longest lasting division among the Left (Gomez et al. 2016: 352) but also within the Communist party family (von Beyme 1985). The communist movement formerly were differentiated as "reformist" and "revolutionary" parties (Eley 2010: 229–318; Foster 1990: 307–576). *Reformism* was seen to be both supportive of liberal democracy and reconciled to the capitalist system, whereas *revolutionary* implied a party committed to the overthrow (possibly violent) of both multiparty democracy and capitalism. Still, Bale and Dunphy (2011) argued that this distinction is less helpful at the present time because most western European RLPs and communist parties are thoroughly committed to liberal democracy, even if they criticize it.

In the post-World War II (WWII) period, New Left and Left Socialist parties were created in the western part of Europe around the revolts during the 1960s. They departed ideologically from the more orthodox versions of both social democrat reformism and communist socialism, proposing an alternative democratic socialism and assuming the "new politics" agenda (Gallagher et al. 1995; Lane and Ersson 1987). Even if they were not the only divisions experienced by the western Left (as the Trotskyite and Maoist ruptures attest), the communist and new Left/Left socialist waves of party formation generated RLPs that have been present in many West Europe polities for a long time.

Moreover, the Eurocommunist strategies proposed during the 1970s by a number of western communist parties also blurred the distinction between socialist and communist families (Bale and Dunphy 2011: 271). The ideological evolution of the communist and radical Left post-communist parties further complicated the boundaries between the old communist and Left socialist families and led to the formation of a new and distinct RLP family (Gomez et al. 2016: 352). Overall, says March (2012: 317), the radical Left now is markedly less ideological and more pragmatic than during the Soviet era. Compared with the international communist movement of 30 years ago, radical Left groups have undergone profound de-radicalization.

Petras (2015a) goes a step farther, identifying some in those on the Left as Non-Leftist Left (NLL). This NLL group has emerged because of the specific conditions generated by the current social and economic crisis. Spontaneous, amorphous, "anarchic," extrainstitutional, and "street-centered," the NLL adopted an irreverent style. Essentially an outgrowth of the Indignant Movement, and aimed at the downwardly mobile middle class, the NLL groups (e.g., Podemos and SYRIZA) have appealed to all those disconnected from power by promising to "end austerity" and restore "dignity and respect." Petras further finds that the NLLs use social polarization to build an electoral base, and then claim that their participation in small-scale local struggles is "proof" that they speak to authentic popular aspirations.

The foregoing discussion highlights the complexity of the contemporary radical Left milieu, which Balabanidis (2015a: 47) has aptly described as the "heir of multiple and often conflicting legacies." In addition, he says their historical trajectory leads to the intrinsic heterogeneity of contemporary RLPs and to the distinction between various subsets of parties within this party family. Clearly, the radical Left often seems to be inherently in conflict—having a plan that is constantly in the making. This also is reflected in the various adjectives used to describe this party family: "far," "extreme," "radical," "anti-capitalist," "socialist," "new," "populist," and so on.

Evidently, there are many well-known problems in defining both the term *radical* and *Left* (March and Mudde 2005: 24). Obviously, they are very broad and ambiguous terms, the meanings of which have shifted over time. For example, in contemporary political debate, the Left is used as an umbrella term to encompass socialist politics in all its guises (Holmes and Roder 2012a: 2), and as such, there is plenty of room for disagreement. Nevertheless, despite the preceding, there is in fact relative consensus as to what constitutes the radical Left (March 2012: 315–20). The present study draws on various authors—that is, March and Mudde (2005: 25), March (2011, 2012), and Bale and Dunphy (2011)—to arrive at the following definition of the *radical Left*:

A party to the left of social democracy that rejects the underlying socio-economic structure of contemporary capitalism and its values and practices while advocating for alternative economic and power structures that involve a major redistribution of resources from the existing social and political elites.

This definition, of course, must be tested against actual policies and, arguably, governing provides the hardest test.

Radical Left parties are "Left" in their identification of economic inequity as the basis of existing political and social arrangements, and in their call for collective economic and social rights as their principal agenda (March and Mudde 2005). They are radical because they advocate an orientation towards "root-and-branch" change of the political system, which is a term of Marxian pedigree according to March (2012: 315). What is more, he says that "radical" does not imply marginality (as does the term "far" or "extreme Left"), nor does it imply that the centre-left is not left-wing (as, implicitly does the use of "Left" to denote the RLPs).

The definition implies a clear distinction between RLPs and extreme Left parties, or as Dunphy (2004: 13) calls them, "minimalists" and "maximalists"—alternatively, traditional and new (see Gomez et al. 2016). The RLPs are those parties that want significant and deep-rooted change to the structures that underpin liberal democratic institutions as well as the market-based economic system; whereas extreme Left parties are those that denounce capitalism and view liberal democracy as a sham, rejecting all forms of compromise and accommodation with actors in the prevailing system (Olsen et al. 2010: 5). The latter group resembles the "old" communist category and could be defined as a "hard Left" (borrowing the 2008 classification of "hard" and "soft" Euroscepticism of Szczerbiak and Taggart).

The "hard" Left favours nationalizations and central planning of the economy, demands the dissolution of NATO, and usually advises leaving the EU. The former group (RLPs) could be called a "soft" Left; they are more sympathetic to the new post-material, identity movements. This group favours a Keynesian economic policy that accepts privatization of some sectors of the economy as well as private initiative; they are suspicious of the EU but do not advise withdrawal from it. The RLPs aspire to represent the entire population and not just the working class. Most scholars, however, usually treat these differences as intra-family variations, so this approach is adopted here as well.

Today RLPs do not substantially oppose liberal democracy nor do they condone revolutionary methods (March 2012: 315). They concentrate on short-term, pragmatic goals rather than endlessly debating the nature of the future socialist state, although they do make use of abstract ideological slogans. Their main raison d'être is no longer (r)evolution for socialism, but the preservation and enhancement of the traditional social democratic welfare consensus, protection of worker rights, and redistribution of wealth (Bale and Dunphy 2011: 271).

The RLPs are internationalist in outlook, expressing solidarity with oppressed people all around the world, and they aim to put themselves in the vanguard of opposition to globalization, neo-liberalism, and imperialism. Their version of anti-capitalism though does not clarify an alternative socialist model, whereas their proposal of radical change refers not only to the economy but also to some key features of contemporary political systems—for example, democracy and accountability (Gomez et al. 2016: 353). The majority also incorporate feminist and Green platforms.

Even though the current European radical Left is a "mosaic Left," the most successful of these parties in terms of electoral gains—of which the <u>Progressive Party of Working People</u> (AKEL) and the Coalition of the Radical Left (SYRIZA) are very good examples—are the less "extreme" and the less "ideologized" RLPs (March 2012: 315) (Table 1.1). Although inviting radicalism it simultaneously nullifies it via various consensus-enhancing mechanisms. This is inextricably linked with the way the EU has developed, especially in the post-1990 era (see next section). The European Union is increasingly perceived as the most significant factor influencing RLPs' policies and strategic choices in national arenas, as well as the principal domain where power struggles unfold in contemporary Europe. Consequently, there are many who consider an RLPs' stance towards the EU as an indicator of their ideological orientation. It has also been an important distinguishing axis within the RLP family, and historically, an ideologically loaded debate.

The EU as a Battlefield

European integration has led to increased polarity among and within similar parties. This is especially true for parties of the Left, which historically have opposed the EU. When analyzing the RLPs' stance on European integration, comparative political science usually uses the lenses of (hard or soft) Euroscepticism (e.g., see Szczerbiak and Taggart 2008). Their negative or skeptical position is not unjustified. As Hooghe et al. note:

> The EU is the product of party–political actors on the Centre-Right, Centre, and to a lesser extent, the Centre-Left who have dominated decision making in Europe during the past half century. European integration is primarily a market-liberal project mitigated by some measure of regulated capitalism. The Euroscepticism of these parties arises not only from their opposition to EU policies but also because they reject the ideology of the EU's construction. (2002: 969)

Table 1.1 The European RLPs Universe

Country	Party	Average vote 2000–2015 (%)[a]	Ideology[b]	Soft or hard Euroscepticism	Government participation after dissolution of the USSR
Austria	KPO (Communist Party of Austria)	0.85	Reform Communism	Soft	No
Cyprus	AKEL (Progressive Party of the Working People)	32.83	Reform Communism	Soft	Yes
Czech Republic	KSCM (Communist Party of Bohemia and Moravia)	14.37	Reform Communism	Soft	No
Denmark	EL (Red-Green Alliance)	4.5	Democratic Socialist	Hard	No
Finland	VAS (Left Alliance)	8.5	Democratic Socialist	Soft	Yes
France	PCF (French Communist Party)	5.34	Reform Communism	Soft	Yes
Germany	LP (Left Party) – previously Party of Democratic Socialism	9.73	Populist Socialist	Soft	No
Greece	KKE (Communist Party of Greece)	6.4	Conservative Communist	Hard	No
Greece	SYRIZA Coalition of the Radical Left	16.38	Populist Socialist	Soft	Yes
Iceland	VG (Left-Green Movement) – previously People' Alliance	13.87	Democratic Socialist	Hard	Yes
Italy	PRC (Party of Communist Refoundation)	4.02	Reform Communism	Soft	Yes

(*continued*)

Table 1.1   (continued)

Country	Party	Average vote 2000–2015 (%)[a]	Ideology[b]	Soft or hard Euroscepticism	Government participation after dissolution of the USSR
Italy	PdCI (Party of Italian Communists) – currently Communist Party of Italy	2.32	Reform Communism	Soft	No
Luxemburg	LENK (The Left)	3.36	Democratic Socialist	Hard	No
Netherlands	SP (Socialist Party)	9.66	Democratic socialist	Soft	No
Norway	SV (Socialist Left Party) – previously Socialist People's Party	7.9	Democratic Socialist	Soft	Yes
Portugal	PCP (Communist Party of Portugal)	7.74	Reform Communist[d]	Soft[d]	No
Portugal	BE (Left Bloc) – previously Democratic Popular Union	6.86	Democratic socialist	Soft	No
Slovakia	KSS (Communist Party of Slovakia)	2.93	Conservative Communist	Hard	No
Spain	PCE (Communist Party of Spain)	4.98[e]	Reform Communism	Soft	No (support)
Spain	Podemos	20.7[c]	Populist Socialist	Soft	No
Sweden	V (Left Party)	6.4	Democratic Socialist	Hard	No (support)
Scotland	SSP (Scottish Socialist Party)	2.56	Populist Socialist	Soft	No

[a]Concerns their electoral record in national parliamentary elections

[b]Based on March's (2011) categorization (partially adjusted)

[c]It took part only in one national election (2015)

[d]Until 2013 the PCP was characterized as a hard Eurosceptic party (March 2011, 2012; Almeida 2012). However, this has been changing in the last couple of years with the party giving a vote of confidence to the Socialist Party's government early in 2015 and following a rift with the Greek KKE

[e]Since 1985 the PCE participates in the national elections under the umbrella of the United Left (IU)

The EU, as a project of negative market-liberal integration, seems fundamentally unreceptive to radical Left policy goals, at least for some RLPs. This concurs with factual developments in the EU, where its successive treaties have exhibited a strong neo-liberal streak throughout the 1990s and 2000s (e.g., Holmes and Roder 2012b: 269–270; Hermann 2009). In this regard, any attempt at radical change is rather futile (Mair 2007). Others on the Left, however, have hailed European integration as the most appropriate means for the Left to realize its goals (Holmes and Lightfoot 2007). This group argues that the Left will have a better chance of effecting any type of change if battles are fought at the EU-level rather than in the national arenas and also will be strengthened by multicountry alliances. Therefore, the most important question is whether accepting the EU frame compromises the RLPs' struggle against the neo-liberal character of the "actually existing EU."

To clarify things, it might be useful to examine the European integration project on two levels; for this analysis I draw on the Holmes and Roder (2012a: 5–7) investigation of this topic, which considered three distinct levels: (1) as a broad normative ideal, (2) as a specific institutional framework, and (3) as a set of specific economic and social policies. The simpler differentiation here combines the latter two dimensions and distinguishes between support for Europeanism as an ideal and support for the "really existing EU." Support for the "ideal EU" reflects acknowledgment and respect for a set of values thought to represent the best of Europe's spiritual and social heritage: social justice, tolerance, solidarity, unity, equality, and so forth. At the same time, it represents a solid belief that an alternative Europe can actually be realized. As such, it encompasses a broad normative ideal—a principled behaviour. At this level most RLPs generally agree.

Support for the EU as it exists today views the European integration project as a specific institutional arrangement and a decision- and policy-making mechanism. RLPs find a number of EU features to be problematic, including the unelected European Commission (EC), the lack of transparency, the democratic deficit at all levels, the neo-liberal class bias, and others. Thus, they do not actually accept the "actually existing EU" nor do they challenge it; rather they view it as an arena for realizing their socialist ambitions. This approach points to the belief that, although the EU is not really a very successful venture, there is no alternative, and therefore that RLPs should work within the EU to transform it. Arguably, it is a question of nuance; that is, most, if not all, RLPs in the EU belong in the first category. It is possible, however, to plainly see a distinction when their actions rather than words are considered.

A further distinction, as proposed by Quaglia (2012), also might be helpful. Even though he speaks of the Italian Left when he posits a distinction between a social Europe, a political Europe, and an economic Europe, his analysis can apply to the Left across Europe as well. In this categorization, it is clear that in general RLPs support "social" Europe and pursue European cooperation in order to formulate common policies and strategies that promote the rights of labour, women, and the environment; however, they oppose a "political" Europe (i.e., greater federalization), a "military" Europe (i.e., development of a common foreign and defense policy), and a "market" Europe (i.e., unhindered competition and loss of national economic levers).

The RLPs also promote measures that will "democratize" the EU and make its institutions and decision making more transparent and closer to the people. Yet beyond this there is little consensus, and it is difficult for the radical Left to move from a defensive to a more positive position (Lightfoot 2012: 20; Holmes and Roder 2012b: 273; March 2008: 12).

Radical left initiatives, in general and despite governing potential, are quite divided at the European level, although a number of competing and overlapping initiatives that attempted to find a common European agenda beyond the lowest common denominator (Almeida 2012: 69; March 2008: 16). The profound, long-standing divisions within the communist movement have been transferred (albeit to a lesser extent) to the radical Left party family, and they help explain why the European Parliamentary Political Group/European United Left/Nordic Green Left (GUE/NGL) and the Party of the European Left (EL) are still less than the sum of their parts (March 2012: 335). The origins of both groups lie in the Communist and Allies Group that emerged in the European Parliament in 1973 and, as of mid-2016, they represent the most important areas of cooperation at the European level for RLPs.

A number of issues associated with the GUE/NGL group and the EL highlight the problems within the radical Left party family with regard to European integration. Some parties that sit in the GUE/NGL group, for example, are not members of the EL or only have observer status (Hanley 2008: 153). The issue for some parties, particularly the Greek Communist Party (KKE) that exited the GUE/NGL in 2014, is that they feel that acceptance of the EL requires accepting the EU as a body of institutions, especially because EL finances rely on the EU budget. There is also the concern that EL membership compromises individual party autonomy (Lightfoot 2012: 21; Katsourides 2012: 199).

If we shift the focus of our comparative analysis from the macro-level of the radical Left party family to the level of its member parties, an even more complex picture emerges. Some of these parties—for example, SYRIZA, the German Left Party (Die Linke), Communist Party of France (PCF), and others—view the European Union as a basis for their own political action that should not be fundamentally called into question, to which they basically have a positive relationship, while others (e.g., the KKE) totally reject the EU (Janssen 2013). Essentially, some RLPs view it as an opportunity while others see the EU as a threat. Debates about the EU are inseparable from the severe economic crisis and a new, more authoritarian and coercive, manifestation of the Europeanization process, which in turn is what brought the issue of governance to the RLPs' agenda again.

AN OLD PUZZLE RESURFACING: COERCIVE EUROPEANIZATION AND AUSTERITARIANISM

Although Europeanization is a fashionable concept, it is also a contested one. The term is used to describe a variety of phenomena and processes of change initiated by the European integration project (Olsen 2002; Kassim 2000), but it is most useful for understanding the dynamics of the evolving European polity. As such, it encompasses a two-way process of change: bottom-up, from the member states to the EU, and top-down, from the EU to the national level (Ladrech 2010); the focus here is on the latter.

European integration progressed through two distinct phases before the Great Recession (Kompsopoulos and Chasoglou 2014: 90)—the Keynesian, anti-Communist phase and the neo-liberal phase. The first phase, which primarily sought economic integration for political reasons, began in 1951 with the European Coal and Steel Community. Although economic integration was based on free-trade guidelines, in the broad sense member states continued to control and regulate their own economic development. This process began to change during the 1980s, with significant milestones being the Single European Act (1986) and the Maastricht Treaty (1992). Since then, political competencies increasingly have been shifted from member states to European governing bodies, especially the Council of the EU (Council of Ministers) and the European Commission. The creation of the Eurozone meant the loss of monetary policy sovereignty, which magnified the asymmetries between the stronger and weaker EU economies.

These institutionalized governance mechanisms were viewed in the late 1990s as elements of a "disciplinary neo-liberalism" and "new constitutionalism" (Gill 1998). Even then, a tendency towards more authoritarian forms of governance—bypassing parliaments and the power of nationally based unions—was visible. The main focus, however, was "negative integration"; that is, removing member states' regulation of the free movement of capital, people, commodities, and services (Kompsopoulos and Chasoglou 2014: 92).

There is currently a new phase of European integration, whereby European governance was attempting to eliminate institutional differences of national capitalism in favour of a single, neo-liberal mode of governance for all EU member states (Gouliamos 2014; Hopner and Schafer 2010). However, instead of the "one-size-fits-all," the situation became "one-size-fits-none" because of the institutional incapacity of monetary policy to respond to the specifics of countries and their situations (Offe 2015: 26; Scharpf 2011). To this end, we can see a clear-cut centralization of power and decision making within the EU's executive organs; in other words, a shift in governance from the national to the supranational level. This type of governance entails a strong class bias (Kompsopoulos and Chasoglou 2014: 93); working people in many European countries still have some organizational and bargaining power at the nation–state level, yet they lack such power at the European level.

The most radical expression of "coercive Europeanization" is the Troika, a supranational body comprised of the International Monetary Fund (IMF), the European Commission, and the European Central Bank (ECB); the Troika is an institution not specified nowhere in any European treaty. European Union member states that were unable to meet their financial commitments and were in need of European assistance to avoid bankruptcy—and to prevent a major impact on European financial systems, including possible chain reactions—were forced to comply with the Troika directives.

This new status quo has been labelled "austeritarianism," and been described as "encompassing the extensive violation of national constitutional rule and parliamentary procedures, the decisive role of unelected and uncontrolled bodies, and widespread violation of popular and national sovereignty" (Bournous and Karatsioubanis 2014). The neo-liberal strategy therefore has shifted from consensus to authoritarian enforcement and blackmail (Offe 2015: 116–117): "[A]ny refusal to adopt austerity measures and other "reforms" will be punished by the refusal of assistance on which recipients existentially depend."

The severe austerity policies were not only destroying welfare states but also were encouraging authoritarian and anti-democratic practices (Amin 2012)—for example, the fierce repression of demonstrations by the police in Greece and Spain. The escalation of the crisis in the Eurozone produced spectacular upheavals in the political landscape. The installation of Papademos in Greece and Monti in Italy were considered by some as "bloodless coups," conceived and administered by Eurozone leaders and bankers (Kouvelakis 2011: 17).

This situation seems to resemble what Poulantzas (1970; revised in 2006) referred to as a "state of exception": a condition of unusual political crisis where the ruling classes invoke an extraordinary situation that allegedly endangers the "common interest" (e.g., the risk of bankruptcy) to justify extraordinary measures that violate collective and individual rights. The Memorandums imposed on Greece and Cyprus using this rationale in fact constituted a mechanism of constitutional aberration; the two countries' parliaments were reduced to mere validating bodies that were forced to accept decisions made by others, which led to feelings of humiliation, indignation, and anger.

This authoritarian turn goes hand in hand with the global economic crisis, which resulted in deep and escalating instability in economic, political, and social spheres all over the world. The EU, in particular, went into severe recession early in 2008, bringing about "the sharpest contraction in the history of the European Union" (European Commission 2009). Many signs suggest that the crisis has deepened the dividing lines separating EU member states (i.e., both East and West divides and North and South divides) and the perception that a positive-sum game has been transformed into a zero-sum frame (Offe 2015: 73). Several reports have pointed out the devastating impact of the economic crisis on the people of Europe and especially those living in South Europe, with extremely destabilizing consequences for their national political systems (Verney and Bosco 2012).

Although the crisis fundamentally has not changed dominant economic or political paradigms, it arguably provided a fertile environment for RLPs (Bruff 2014; March and Rommerskirchen 2015). In the face of increasing economic uncertainty, rising unemployment, and reduced wages and social benefits, RLPs were expected to benefit politically primarily because they advised a change in economic structures and models (Dunphy 2004); many proposed substantive alternatives to the pro-market economy that has dominated advanced industrial democracies. In fact, a number of

European RLPs have seen their electoral share rise—for example, SYRIZA, the Dutch Socialist Party (SP), and the Danish Red-Green Alliance (EL) (Gomez et al. 2016: 351).

In addition, the economic crisis has revealed the inability of European social democracy to take advantage of a situation that on the surface appears tailor-made for a critical view of free market capitalism (Bruff 2014: 114). The impact of the economic situation, as well as the discrediting of "Third Way" social democracy, have led some analysts to propose the so-called "vacuum thesis," which claims that the neo-liberalization of social democracy has allowed RLPs to flourish (Lavelle 2008). The radical Left thus has been becoming the principal challenge to mainstream social democratic parties, in large part because its main parties are no longer extreme; rather, they present themselves as defending the values and policies that social democrats have allegedly abandoned—for example, public ownership and economic interventionism (March 2008: 9–10; see also Cronin et al. 2011).

Still, "reality has often confounded prognosis, with electoral dividends from the Great Recession meagre, and every success counteracted by an apparent debacle" (March 2015; see also Holmes and Roder 2012b: 276). Certainly, politically it is the Right and austerity programs that have dominated responses to the crisis, leading to suspicions that the radical Left had passed up a perfect opportunity to exploit capitalism's travails. The end result of the RLPs' inability to act was a neo-liberal economic and cultural hegemony that, according to some scholars, represents the cause of the crisis (Lapavitsas 2014; Schmidt and Thatcher 2014; Bruff 2014).

Lyrintzis (2011: 18) posed an intriguing question: "[W]hy in a period of economic crisis and austerity do the ideas of the Left about equality, social justice and solidarity not appeal to the masses?" Tentative explanations include the following: the incompetency of the political agents of the Left to convincingly represent the ideals of it, the ideological defeat of the Left on a European level, and its inability to present coherent proposals beyond abstract and vague rhetoric. History, argues Lyrintzis (2011: 22), shows that in times of economic crisis societies often prefer conservative rather than radical political formations (see also March and Mikhaylov 2014; Burnham 2011; Gamble 2009: 112).

Likewise, Petras (2015a) theorizes this conservatism through the analytical prism of "middle-class radicalism." The radicalized middle class, says Petras, includes the social strata who aspired to and who, until recently, experienced upward mobility but have now found their path blocked by the austerity programs imposed by right-wing as well as social democratic parties. Frustrated by the social democrats' "betrayal" and facing downward mobility, the radicalized middle-class objective was to restore their past access to social advancement and prosperity. For this group, the communist Left was too radical because it sought to overturn capitalism and too distant itself from power to effect change. They therefore turned to the new Left—the radical Left.

Despite the perceived inability of the Left to capitalize on the crisis, however, the two parties under study have managed to appeal effectively to the masses. Moreover, both parties were elected to office, and SYRIZA even amid the huge economic crisis. Therefore, a more interesting question would be: "[W]hat have these two parties done differently than other RLPs that enabled them to increase their (or maintain the already high) electoral strength and also take part in government?" The following are other interesting questions to consider regarding the impact of the economic crisis on their programmes and their ideology: Does the crisis lead to increased radicalization or moderation? Does social immiseration lead to political radicalism? What role does the government-opposition dynamics play in this process? These questions touch on the strategy of RLPs.

The resulting debates have often led to deep and paralyzing divisions among leftists (Spourdalakis 2013). One leftist group suggested that severe crises are conducive to radical social transformation. Other factions of the Left argue that if it has learned anything from the history of economic crises it is that inadequate or uninspiring responses to those crises have led to political ineffectiveness, as well as huge political and ideological defeats. Arguably, the recent and ongoing economic crisis has revitalized this discussion among many in the radical Left. The severity and the longevity of the global capitalist crisis have been forcing the RLPs to focus their strategy on this issue.

Increasingly, the RLPs fight against austerity and neo-liberalism relates to the Left's standing and strategy on the matter of government participation. This strategy naturally varies according to several factors: the overall historical setting; factors specific to the region, the country, the culture, the structure of political opportunity; the balance of power between social and political forces; and the history of each political party, as well as other party-specific factors. Although governing within the EU implies an acknowledgment that "the basic conditions for government participation have been established by neo-liberalism and are not easily changed," at the same time "the Left faces the challenge of using the opportunity [i.e., the economic crisis] to fight for the fulfilment of a just society" (Daiber and Kulke 2010: 7, 9).[1]

A Frame of Analysis

Radical Left parties traditionally have been seen as highly ideological and introverted, as parties that concentrated on policy purity to the exclusion of electoral success and government participation. This is still very much the case for those parties that wish to avoid disputes over programme strategy and the compromises that are necessary to govern successfully. These parties (e.g., the KKE) seemed to prefer a niche position, as they focus on ideology and reject compromises of government. This position may guarantee stability but offered the party little influence (March 2012: 331). Other RLPs (e.g., AKEL) have long aimed primarily at expanding their electorate and attaining national offices (Katsourides 2012; Dunphy and Bale 2007).

Whereas prior to 1989 RLP government participation was very rare, beginning in 1990 and until 2012, 17 RLPs joined or gave legislative support to governments (March and Rommerskirchen 2015). We can see that as the broad Left became more fragmented, RLP government participation became more commonplace (Bale and Dunphy 2011) because the strategies that they adopted reflected ambition and a realistic possibility to govern. According to Brie, RLPs seemed to view governing under a new perspective; that is, as a project of transformation whereby the party must find a position midway between traditional reformist politics and the orthodox concept of revolution in order to influence national politics (2010: 25).

This perspective is not the work of RLPs' leadership alone. Given the impoverishment of the working classes and other popular strata that the Left claims to politically represent as a result of the economic crisis, there was also a bottom-up realization that the Left's traditional defensive strategies were inadequate. Therefore, many RLPs chose government participation as a way to help protect the interests of the less privileged rather than patiently waiting for the right conditions. In turn, this also influenced party positions toward the EU, internal affairs, possible allies, and so on.

With this new conceptualization of government participation adopted by some RLPs, the "vote-office-policy" framework (Strom 1990; Muller and Strom 1999) is a helpful perspective through which to assess their strategic choices—choices that open the way for them to seize an opportunity to influence national politics. As RLPs are increasingly aligned with liberal democracy and become more commonplace political actors (Bale and Dunphy 2011), this framework is now more often used to interpret and analyze their behaviour; this is a clear indication of how the RLPs have changed since earlier times. Some interesting questions in this regard include the following: Why and how do Left parties enter government? What do they actually do when they get there? What happens to them once they step down from office? (Olsen et al. 2010: 2–3). Can they succeed without recanting their core ideology?

Using this model, and considering a party's stipulated objectives, it is possible to distinguish between vote-seeking, office-seeking, and policy-seeking models of party behaviour (Strom 1990). Parties that can be classified as vote-seeking try to maximize their electoral support as a way to control government; in this way, they are also vote maximizers. Office-seeking parties aim to maximize their control over political office; that is, they engage in the pursuit of government portfolios often over and above their electoral or policy value. Finally, the policy-seeking party looks to maximize its effect on public policy through coalitions with parties that espouse similar policies. The policy-seeking model assumes that office is to be pursued in an instrumental manner to facilitate the implementation of favourable public policies (Budge and Laver 1986).

Despite the criticism the vote-office-policy model has received (see summary in Strom 1990: 568–570), it still remains a useful analytical tool. Most notably, the three goals need not be mutually exclusive. For instance, a party may pursue a policy position that is also electorally optimal. Policy influence and office benefits are often compatible goals because government incumbency provides both. Nevertheless, at any given time a party generally will prioritize one specific goal (Harmel and Kenneth 1994), assessing the trade-offs inherent in the three models. For example, although policy influence and office benefits may be compatible goals, when a government coalition is involved, often each party strikes its own bargains with regard to policy and portfolios (Strom 1990: 572).

Another trade-off concerns the relationship between seeking office and seeking votes because party behaviour in office may affect a party's subsequent performance at the polls (Laver 2008)—most often negatively. This occurs because the populace judges the governing parties more harshly than the opposition, especially when looking for consistency between promise and performance.

Additional factors are involved in party strategy; for example, there is the party leader's influence and autonomy vis-à-vis the party organization (Katz and Mair 1993). Leaders are thought to be more office-oriented than party activists and the electorate because the perceived personal benefits of holding office (Laver 1981). In addition, once in office, leaders often draw away from collective decision making, which they see as constraining. Greater involvement in the institutions of government also may mean heavy dependence on those party leaders appointed to cabinet offices or elected to a presidency (Dunphy and Bale 2011). These leaders may find themselves less tolerant of internal criticism about policy or presentation of shortcomings.

Party leaders, however, do not act without checks; they are constrained by party organization, by coalition partners, and by the electorate. For example, if their party is more labour-intense than capital-intense, the leaders find it more difficult to chart an autonomous course. Parties of the Left are generally more labour-intense and usually (more) dependent on activists who are more interested in policy than office benefits. This situation can cause tension between activists and the leadership because, although governing parties can control larger resources and therefore dispense more benefits to party activists, this does not always suffice as activists tend to be driven by ideology (Bale and Dunphy 2011: 275).

Most political parties navigate between these goals and, increasingly, the RLPs behave no differently (Bale and Dunphy 2011: 271). However, once RLPs decide to decisively influence political life, they must give priority to office-seeking goals, which leads to the need for vote maximization, both of which in turn lead to deemphasizing policy objectives consistent with their ideology—at least in its purest form. For example, if they want to become legitimate coalition partners, they must restructure or dilute policy commitments (Olsen et al. 2010: 9). Many RLPs see government participation as a way to exert greater influence over national policies and a logical step towards their full acceptance as legitimate actors with full democratic credentials. Although the goal of achieving legitimacy can be considered as a target outside the familiar triad, it also can be viewed as a tool for becoming coalitionable and therefore a potential partner in office.

SELECTION OF CASE STUDIES AND THE BOOK'S SCOPE AND METHODOLOGY

AKEL and SYRIZA were selected as case studies for several reasons. First, both parties clearly belong to the radical Left party family (i.e., they are both members of the GUE/NGL); more important, they are undoubtedly the most prominent RLPs in Europe as of mid-2016. Second, the two parties' countries are similar culturally (e.g., common language and religion) and also have analogous historical patterns of late development and authoritarianism. Third, Cyprus and Greece have experienced severe economic upheaval and unrest because of the widespread economic crisis. Finally, both parties have expressed their government aspirations and, more importantly, both have had their leaders elected to executive offices.

AKEL and SYRIZA are the only two RLPs that have led governments in post-war Europe and this places significant added value on their comparative study. Moreover, and contrary to most RLPs experience as junior coalition partners, AKEL and SYRIZA have been dominant government partners or have governed alone (AKEL), thus increasing their ability for policy impact. Both parties assumed government responsibilities, albeit for different reasons and at different times.

Their similarities must not be overstated, however, since SYRIZA and AKEL differ considerably in terms of (ideological) trajectory, party origins, and organization, as well as country traditions. AKEL represents the more orthodox (i.e., pragmatic) communists within the radical Left milieu, whereas SYRIZA represents the less orthodox and mostly Eurocommunist version. Even though following different trajectories, they have faced similar challenges in their transformation to governing parties. Besides, their political and party systems also differ significantly. The main differences are highlighted in this book and are of particular importance because they offer an analytical leverage to explain the outcomes—two different RLPs in government, similar results.

This book goes beyond the paradigm that emphasizes the exceptionality of each country or party under study. While pointing to the parties' special circumstances, it tries to link developments in both countries and parties with wider European debates. The chapters here try to explain each party's course by focusing on various aspects and levels of study; that is, the historical paths that demarcate their political and ideological "DNA" and organizational traditions, the de-legitimization of other actors that reflect changes in the structure of political opportunity, and so forth. At the same time the book takes into serious consideration the political actor itself; that is, agency is just as important as the processes.

Analysis therefore is conducted according to the paradigm of parties as both independent and dependent actors within the political system.

This line of analysis places significant emphasis on the institution of political parties per se (Mair 1997: 89; Sartori 1990: 178). Parties, in this regard, are considered to be purposive actors, and that they are in a position to shape at least some of the parameters within which they operate. This is more applicable to the parties to the Left of mainstream social democracy, which Dunphy (2004) describes as "transformatory" parties.

An attempt has been made here to provide a more complete understanding of the radical Left party family by examining in detail two of its most prominent exponents. The book is meant to open the way to further research into a number of related issues such as the impact of EU politics on national arenas and vice versa, the impact of the economic crisis on political parties' programmes, and the thin lines involved in issues of party identities.

The book is divided into seven chapters including an introduction and conclusion. This introductory chapter has considered reasons for the radical Left's resurgence as a possible governing actor during the past 10 years, has examined the various definitions and degrees of the "Left," and has provided the analytical framework for this study. In Chap. 2 the historical and theoretical issues associated with the Left's participation in government are detailed, while Chaps. 3 and 4 focus on the historical evolution of the two parties. Chapter 5 emphasizes the developments and circumstances that led to the RLPs rise to power, and Chap. 6 contains an overview and analysis of their government experiences. Unavoidably, the chapters touch on the issue of radical Left de-radicalization vis-à-vis governing prospects and strategies. In the concluding chapter, there is a discussion of the broader issue of what to expect when radical leftists achieve governance or when they are in a position to claim government participation.

The election of SYRIZA and AKEL party members to government and the questions, dilemmas, and challenges that poses, not only for Greece and Cyprus but also for the entire EU and the RLP family, are issues of significant academic and political interest. The topics will require more detailed examination and further analysis. Both parties' experience in government can provide an analytic example that is informative of the wider experience of RLPs' participation in (coalition) governments. The communist and other Left parties' perceptions of government participation, however, predate the most recent economic crisis and never have been related solely to (economic) crises; Chapter 2 focuses on these issues.

NOTE

1. The Daiber and Kulke (2010) volume is a collection of essays representing work of the most important RLP research foundations in Europe and in Latin America. The introduction summarizes the common threads of their arguments.

BIBLIOGRAPHY

Almeida, D. (2012). *The Impact of European Integration on Political Parties – Beyond the Permissive Consensus*, Oxon: Routledge.

Amin, S. (2012). 'Implosion of the European System', *Review of the Month*, 64 (4), September.

Balabanidis, Y. (2015a). 'Radical Left, the Heir of Many Ancestors', *Sygxrona Themata*, 130–131 (December), pp. 46–50 [in Greek].

Bale, T. and Dunphy, R. (2011). 'In From the Cold? Left Parties and Government Involvement Since 1989', *Comparative European Politics*, 9(3), pp. 269–291.

Bell, D.S., (Ed.) (1993). *Western European Communists and the Collapse of Communism*, Oxford, UK: Berg Publishers.

von Beyme, K. (1985). *Political Parties in Western Democracies*. New York, NY: St. Martin's Press.

Boggs, C. (1995). *The Socialist Tradition: From Crisis to Decline*, London: Routledge.

Bosco, A. (2001). 'Four Actors in Search of a Role: The Southern European Communist Parties', in N. Diamandouros and R. Gunther (Eds), *Parties, Politics and Democracy in the New Europe*, Baltimore: John Hopkins University Press.

Botella, J. and Ramiro, L. (Eds.) (2003). *The Crisis of Communism and Party Change: The Evolution of West European Communist and Post-Communist Parties*, Barcelona: Institut of Ciencies Politiques i Socials.

Bournous, Y. and Karatsioubanis, Y. (2014). 'Austerity, Collapse, and the Rise of the Radical Left in Greece', *New Politics*, XV(2), http://newpol.org/content/austerity-collapse-and-%E2%80%A8rise-radical-left-greece, Accessed 15 May 2015.

Brie, M. (2010). 'Is Socialist Politics Possible in Government? Five Objections by Rosa Luxemburg and Five Offers for a Discussion', in Daiber, B. (Eds.) *The Left in Government. Latin America and Europe Compared*, Brussels: Rosa Luxemburg Foundation, pp. 21–34.

Bruff, I. (2014). 'The Rise of Authoritarian Neoliberalism', *Rethinking Marxism*, 26(1), pp. 113–129.

Budge, I. and Laver, M. (1986). 'Office Seeking and Policy Pursuit in Coalition Theory', *Legislative Studies Quarterly*, 11, pp. 485–506.

Bull, M.J. and Heywood, P. (Eds). (1994). *West European Communist Parties after the Revolutions of 1989*, Basingstoke: Macmillan.

Burnham, P. (2011). 'Towards a Political Theory of Crisis: Policy and Resistance across Europe', *New Political Science*, 33(4), pp. 493–507.

Cronin, J., Ross, G., and Shoch, J. (2011). 'Introduction: The New World of the Centre-Left', in J. Cronin, G. Ross, and J. Shoch (Eds), *What's Left of the Left: Democrats and Social Democrats in Challenging Times*, London: Duke University Press.

Daiber, B. and Kulke, R. (2010). 'Introduction', in Daiber, B. (Eds.) *The Left in Government. Latin America and Europe Compared*, Brussels: Rosa Luxemburg Foundation, pp. 7–20.

Dunphy, R. (2007). 'In Search of an Identity: Finland's Left Alliance and the Experience of Coalition Government', *Contemporary Politics* 13(1), pp. 37–55.

Dunphy, R. (2004). *Contesting Capitalism – Left Parties and European Integration*, Manchester: Manchester University Press.

Dunphy, R. and Bale, T. (2011). 'The radical left in coalition government: Towards a comparative measurement of success and failure', *Party Politics*, 17(4), pp. 488–504.

Dunphy, R., and Bale, T. (2007). 'Red flag still flying?', *Party politics*, 13 (3), pp. 129–146.

Eley, G. (2010). *Forging Democracy: The History of the Left in Europe*, Savvalas: Athens [in Greek].

Elff, M. (2013), 'On the Distinctiveness of Party Families', Paper prepared for t the 71th Annual Conference of the Midwest Political Science Association, Palmer House Hilton, Chicago, Illinois, April 11–14.

European Commission (2009). *Economic Crisis in Europe: Causes, Consequences and Responses*, EUROPEAN ECONOMY 7|2009, http://ec.europa.eu/economy_finance/publications/publication15887_en.pdf.

Foster, W. (1990). *History of the Three Internationals*, Athens: Gnoseis.

Gamble, A. (2009). *The Spectre at the Feast: Capitalist Crisis and the Politics of Recession*, Basingstoke: Palgrave.

Gallagher, M., Laver, M. and P. Mair (1995). *Representative Government in Modern Europe: Institutions, Parties and Governments*. Boston, MA: McGraw Hill.

Gill, S. (1998). 'European Governance and New Constitutionalism: Economic and Monetary Union and Alternatives to Disciplinary Neoliberalism in Europe', *New Political Economy*, 3 (1).

Gomez, R. Morales, L. and Ramiro, L. (2016). 'Varieties of Radicalism: Examining the Diversity of Radical Left Parties and Voters in Western Europe, *West European Politics*, 39(2), pp. 351–379.

Gouliamos, C. (2014). *The Monstrous Idol of Europe*, Athens: Modern Horizons [in Greek].

Hanley, D. (2008). *Beyond the Nation State*, Basingstoke: Palgrave Macmillan.

Harmel, R., and Kenneth, J. (1994). An integrate theory of party goals and party change. *Journal of Theoretical Politics*, 6 (4), pp. 259–287.

Hermann, C. (2009). 'Neoliberalism in the EU", *Studies in Political Economy*, Vol. 79, pp. 61–89.

Holmes M. and Roder K. (2012a). 'The Left from Laaken to Lisbon', in M. Holmes and K. Roder (Eds). *The Left and the European Constitution. From Laaken to Lisbon*, Manchester: Manchester University Press, pp. 1–17.

Holmes M. and Roder K. (2012b). 'The Left and European Integration beyond Lisbon', in M. Holmes and K. Roder (Eds). *The Left and the European Constitution. From Laaken to Lisbon*, Manchester: Manchester University Press, pp. 269–277.

Holmes, M. and Lightfoot, S. (2007). 'The Europeanisation of Left Political Parties: Limits to Adaptation and Consensus', *Capital and Class*, 93, pp. 101–119.

Hooghe, L., Marks, G. and Wilson, C. (2002). 'Does left/right Structure Party Positions on European Integration?', *Comparative Political Studies*, 35(8), pp. 965–989.

Hopner, M. and Schafer, A. (2010). 'A New Phase of European Integration: Organised Capitalisms in Post-Ricardian Europe', *West European Politics*, 33 (2), pp. 344–368.

Janssen, T. (2013). *The Parties of the Left in Europe*. Berlin: Rosa Luxembourg Stiftung.

Kassim, H. (2000). 'Conclusion'. In H. Kassim, B.G. Peters and V. Wright (Eds.) *The National Co-ordination of EU Policy*, Oxford: Oxford University Press, pp. 235–264.

Katsourides, Y. (2012). Travelling against the Tide: The Cypriot Communist Left in the Post-1990 Era, *Perspectives on European Politics and Society*, 13 (2), pp. 187–209.

Katz, R., and Mair, P., (1993). 'The Evolution of Party Organizations in Europe: the Three Faces of Party Organization', *Special issue of the American Review of Politics*, 14, pp. 593–617.

Kompsopoulos, J. and Chasoglou, J. (2014). 'The Collapse and Transformation of the Greek Party System', *Socialism and Democracy*, 28(1), pp. 90–112.

Kouvelakis, S. (2011). 'The Greek Cauldron', *New Left Review*, 72, pp. 17–32.

Ladrech, R. (2010). *Europeanization of National Politics*, Basingstoke: Palgrave Macmillan.

Lane, J.-E., and Ersson, S. (1987). *Politics and Society in Western Europe*. London: Sage.

Lapavitsas, C. (2014). *A Radical Programme for Greece and the Periphery of the Eurozone*, Athens: Livanis [in Greek].

Lavelle, A. (2008). *The Death of Social Democracy: Political Consequences in the 21st Century*, Aldershot: Ashgate.

Laver, M. (2008). 'Governmental Politics and the Dynamics of Multiparty Competition', *Political Research Quarterly*, 61(3), pp. 532–536.

Laver, M. (1981). *The Politics of Private Desires*, Harmondsworth: Penguin.

Lightfoot, S. (2012). 'Left Parties at the EU Level: Influencing the Convention', in M. Holmes and K. Roder (Eds), *The Left and the European Constitution. From Laaken to Lisbon*, Manchester: Manchester University Press, pp. 18–34.

Lyrintzis, C. (2011). 'Greek Politics in the Era of Economic Crisis: Reassessing Causes and Effects', Hellenic Observatory Papers on Greece and Southeast Europe, 45.

Mair, P. (2007). 'Political Opposition and the European Union', *Government and Opposition*, 42(1), pp. 1–17.

Mair, P. (1997). *Party System Change: Approaches and Interpretations*, Oxford: Clarendon Press.

Mair, P. and Mudde, C. (1998). 'The Party Family and its Study', *Annual Review of Political Science*, 1, pp. 211–229.

March, L. (2015). 'The European Radical Left Beyond Syriza – a New Left-wing Zeitgeist?', https://epern.wordpress.com/2015/02/27/the-european-radical-left-beyond-syriza-a-new-left-wing-zeitgeist/, accessed, 12 March 2015.

March, L. (2012). 'Problems and Perspectives of Contemporary European Radical Left Parties: Chasing a Lost World or Still a World to Win?', *International Critical Thought*, 2(3), pp. 314–339.

March, L. (2011). *Radical Left Parties in Europe*, London: Routledge.

March, L. (2008). Contemporary Far Left Parties in Europe – From Marxism to the Mainstream? Friedrich Ebert Foundation, November 2008, Berlin: library. fes.de/pdf-files/id/ipa/05818.pdf.

March, L. and Rommerskirchen, C. (2015). 'Out of Left Field? Explaining the Variable Electoral Success of European Radical Left Parties', *Party Politics*, 21(1), pp. 40–53.

March, M. and Mikhaylov, S. (2014). 'A Conservative Revolution: The Electoral Response to Economic Crisis in Ireland', *Journal of Elections, Public Opinion and Parties*, 24(2), pp. 160–179.

March. L., and Mudde, C. (2005). 'What's left of the radical left? The European Radical Left after 1989: Decline and Mutation', *Comparative European Politics*, 3 (1), pp. 23–49.

Moschonas, G. (2010). 'The Electoral Crisis of Social Democracy: The Great Retreat of the European Social Democratic Parties (1950-2009)', Paper presented at the International workshop by Transform! Europe, Palma de Majorca, 12–13 March 2010, http://transform-network.net/uploads/tx_news/MoschonasElectoralSD_01.pdf.

Muller, W. and Strom, K. (1999). *Policy, office, or votes: How political parties in Western Europe make hard decisions* (ch 1), Cambridge: Cambridge University Press.

Offe, K. (2015). *Europe Entrapped*, Cambridge: Polity Press.

Olsen, J., Koß, M., and Hough, D. (2010). 'From Pariahs to Players? Left parties in National Governments. In J. Olsen, M. Koß and D. Hough (eds.) *Left Parties in Government*, New York: Palgrave Macmillan, pp. 1–15.

Olsen, J. P. (2002). 'The Many Faces of Europeanization', *Journal of Common Market Studies*, 40(5), pp 921–952.

Petras, J. (2015a). 'The Radical Reconfiguration of Southern European Politics: The Rise of the Non Leftist Left'. http://petras.lahaine.org/?p=2040, 21 June 2015, Accessed 22 July 2015.

Petras, J. (2015b). 'Syriza: Plunder, Pillage and Prostration. (How the 'Hard Left' embraces the policies of the Hard Right'. http://petras.lahaine.org/?p=2039, 15 June 2015, Accessed 22 July 2015.

Petras (2015c). 'Greek elections: January and September 2015 - From Hope to Fear and Despair', http://petras.lahaine.org/?p=2048, Accessed 1 September 2015.

Quaglia, L. (2012). 'The Left in Italy and the Lisbon Treaty: a "Political" Europe, a "Social" Europe and an "Economic" Europe', in M. Holmes and K. Roder (Eds). The Left and the European Constitution. From Laaken to Lisbon, Manchester: Manchester University Press, pp. 118–135.

Sartori, G. (1990). 'The sociology of parties: a critical review', in P. Mair, (Ed.) *The West European party system*, Oxford: Oxford University Press, pp. 150–184.

Scharpf, F. (2011). 'Monetary Union, Fiscal Crisis and the preemption of Democracy', Max Plank Institute for the Study of Societies, MPifG Discussion Paper 11/11.

Schmidt, V. and Thatcher, M. (2014), 'Why are neoliberal ideas so resilient in Europe's political economy?', *Critical Policy Studies*, 8(3), pp. 340–347.

Spourdalakis, M. (2013), 'Left Strategy in the Greek Cauldron: Explaining SYRIZA's Success', in L. Panitch, G. Albo and V. Chibber (Eds), *Socialist Register 2013: The Question of Strategy*, London: Merlin Press, pp. 98–120.

Strom K. (1990). 'A Behavioural Theory of Competitive Political Parties', *American Journal of Political Science*, 34(2), pp. 565–598.

Szczerbiak, A., and P. Taggart (eds.). 2008. *Opposing Europe? The comparative party politics of Euroscepticism*, Vol. I and II. Oxford: Oxford University Press.

Verney, S. and Bosco, A. (2012), 'Living Parallel Lives: Italy and Greece in an Age of Austerity', *South European Society and Politics*, 18(4), pp. 397–426.

CHAPTER 2

The Left and Power: A Historical Retrospective

Abstract In this chapter I reflect on the historical debates and theoretical issues related to the participation of communist and socialist parties in government. In this regard, it provides a history of the Left stance towards government participation in Europe, a subject of stormy debate since the late nineteenth century. In so doing, I draw not only on (Euro)communist parties' experience but South Europe socialists' as well. The impact of the dissolution of the USSR on the communist parties' strategy also is examined because it represents a milestone in their historical evolution. Finally, the chapter highlights the issues at the heart of these debates.

Keywords Communist parties • Socialist parties • South Europe • Eurocommunism • Government • Strategy

For communist parties, the question of strategy, or "the road to power," has been a matter of controversy since the days of Marx. More so than other political parties, the Left parties have historically struggled with the question of how to approach parliamentary democracy: to reject it per se as a capitalist farce that in reality represses the working class, or to try to change the system from within, fundamentally reshaping capitalist structures and democratic institutions (Olsen et al. 2010: 11). Communist parties, however, have differentiated between "being in power" and "being in government" and the more recent radical Left parties (RLPs) also seem to be aware of this distinction (e.g., see Iliada 2010: 47).

© The Editor(s) (if applicable) and The Author(s) 2016   27
Y. Katsourides, *Radical Left Parties in Government*,
DOI 10.1057/978-1-137-58841-8_2

Certain questions have always been at the heart of such debates, including the following:

- Revolution or evolution?
- Peaceful, parliamentary road to socialism or violent revolutionary rupture with capitalism?
- Transforming or crushing the bourgeois state?
- Taking part in government or maintaining ideological purity?
- Does holding a governmental office equal having power within the bourgeois state?

The (communist) Left has wavered on these choices/questions throughout the twentieth century and continues to vacillate. These discussions have put a lasting mark on the Left's legacy and still trouble it. The question that always arises is whether taking part in capitalist institutions (e.g., government) can eventually lead to socialism or whether this will unavoidably strengthen the capitalist status quo (Przeworski 1980: 27–28).

The establishment of the USSR following the Russian Revolution gave the world a concrete example of a socialist state. After several failed attempts to replicate its successful revolution, however, the Left recognized that an alternative strategy was necessary. The new strategy, named the "democratic road to socialism," would ensure its rise to power through elections. The first formulations appeared as a variation of the early twentieth-century Marxist social democracy, and these developed into the "united front" strategy against fascism during the 1930s and 1940s. A third reformulation came about as a result of the Eurocommunism project of the 1970s and the fourth through the more recent (1990s and 2000s) pursuits of the modern European Left. Increasingly, however, the strategy of a slow, incremental, and peaceful passage to socialism has prevailed, especially in the post-WWII era.

The most basic argument in favour of this strategy is the perceived inability of the Leninist theory and old-fashioned communist parties to offer an effective socialist strategy for the West. The Leninist strategy has been perceived as one of assaulting and capturing power, a strategy most suited to countries plagued by conditions of poverty and backwardness (Mpelantis 2014: 76–77). The Leninist model also has been seen to take a positive stance towards violence, to harbour an intrinsic hostility towards democracy, and to favour totalitarianism. This model now is thought to be inappropriate for the West with its long history of parliamentarism, and that it may lead to the social and political marginalization of the Left from vital social allies (e.g., the middle classes). The dissolution of the socialist bloc in 1989–1991 reinforced this argument. Moreover, ever since the dismantling of the USSR the Left has not been able to produce a persuasive, alternative social model.

Social and political scientists always examine the past to look for repeated patterns of political behaviour. In the context of this study, it is useful to examine the earlier stances and experiences of the communist Left parties towards government participation and compare these to their present positions and behaviours. On the other hand, we also can gain constructive insight by studying party families close to the communists, the social democrats, and the socialists, arguably much closer in the past than in the present. Throughout the twentieth century social democrats and socialists were always considered part of the wider Left bloc, and this is still true for some. Many scholars and the RLPs themselves, however, now differentiate between the Left and the social democrats and/or the socialists, regarding the latter two as centrist parties that have endorsed liberal values, although to different degrees (March 2011; Wahl 2010; Dunphy 2004).

SOUTH EUROPE SOCIALIST PARTIES AS A PARADIGM

The social democrats and the socialists represented two distinct party families for some time after the communists left the Second International in 1917. The social democrats tended to flourish in northern Europe, whereas the socialists converged in South Europe. The socialist parties were overideologized organizations with weak ties to trade unions and with strong Marxist tendencies; for these reasons they verbally pursued the complete abolishment of capitalism. Their principal objective was modernization and the development of welfare policies. In some instances (e.g., Spain and Greece) they played an important role in the consolidation of democracy (Sassoon 1997: 4).

The social democrats, on the other hand, were more pragmatic; they accommodated many more ideological tendencies and established very strong links to the trade unions. Their task was not the modernization of capitalism but its management and the proper distribution of wealth resulting from growth. Although both party families gradually accepted the basic norms and values of capitalism, this occurred at different times—the socialists much later than the social democrats (Sassoon 1997: 3–6; Diamantopoulos 1991: 69–95). This was not unrelated to the intense competition the former faced from resilient communist parties in South Europe (Smith 2015).

The social democratic move towards more centrist politics and away from leftist positions was increasingly evident during the post-WWII years when they accepted a so-called social market economy (i.e., socially regulated capitalism). Here, socialism was reduced from a major claim for an alternative model of social organization to a moral demand for humanizing capitalism. The seminal work of Giddens (1998), *The Third Way*, and its influence on Tony Blair's New Labour Party completed this transformation. Giddens led the way to the de-labourization of the Labour Party and its dissociation from what he called the "old Left" (i.e., the socialist Left); he argued in favour of rebuilding the party along more liberal and decentralized lines. Those lines were to include: the primacy of the market for fostering growth, the abandonment of the inclusive welfare state for a more selective one, the promotion of individual ethics, the support for globalization, the need for supranationalism, and an open party.

The socialists in South Europe presented a different case. By looking at their historical path, we can find valuable insights into the way these parties dealt with issues similar to those that the RLPs were facing. The 1980s saw the socialist parties of the European south taking on the executive role, with some Eurocommunist parties either partaking in governing coalitions or supporting the socialist governments (see later in chapter). The socialist experiments in South Europe were not social democratic (i.e., accepting capitalism) from the outset. Nonetheless, they gradually became more pragmatic, and during their time in governments they began to make ideological adjustments, indicating the acceptance of a capitalist reality (Mpelantis 2014: 127; Sassoon 1996: 497–644; Diamantopoulos 1991: 75).

We can understand their development and direction by looking at the parties only in the context of society and politics of South Europe. In that area the social, economic, and political development differed dramatically from that in the north; this can partially explain the different trajectories of their political parties (Pinto and Teixeira 2002). Although this hardly indicates backwardness, as argued by some theorists who regard peripheries beyond the European north as vying to catch up with the "developed" and "progressive" north (e.g., Mouzelis 1994), it does suggest a different path of development. Beginning in the 1930s the South Europe countries suffered under dictatorships and authoritative regimes; this led to an intense left–right polarization that radicalized the parties of the (plural) Left and caused their exclusion from the inner-party system (see Bosco 2001, for a review of the concept). Marxism was the defining characteristic of the southern European socialists, and references to social- ism were retained well into the 1980s, indicating that they did not mean to bring about a mere electoral change in government.

Nevertheless, it should be noted that the socialists demanded not only social change but also civil modernization, democratization, and open- ing of the political system to outsiders (i.e., themselves) (Sassoon 1997: 1–16). As such, the South Europe socialist parties promoted a peaceful road to socialism, which they still envisaged as a different society, much like the Eurocommunists. Their programmes resembled those of Allende's Popular Unity and the post-WWII Labour governments in Britain, which undertook extensive nationalization, although they were not the same.

South Europe socialist parties did not immediately raise the idea of changing the fundamental bases of capitalism, but they did question the existing balance between state and private initiative; they still professed socialism and introduced new political personnel into the political system. Despite their anti-capitalist, anti-EEC (European Economic Community), and anti-imperialist rhetoric, however, in practice they were not subver- sive parties. Instead, they focused on the following: small specific changes to democratize state functions and apparatus, which on some occasions led to extensive clientelism (e.g., Greece); a Keynesian economic strategy of increasing demand through more public spending and income redis- tribution, among other things; promoting social equality through larger pensions and better social welfare benefits; and restricting capital unac- countability. None of these parties withdrew its country from the EEC or NATO, and the more time the parties spent in governments, the less radical their policies became (Diamantopoulos 1991: 69–95).

As a result of the economic crisis during the late 1970s and early 1980s, all these parties radically modified their policies, and in quite a similar fash- ion became full-fledged social democratic parties (Sassoon 1996: 112). They all changed their emphasis from the primacy of social justice to the need for economic and social development. At their 1985 Congress, the French Socialist Party (PSF) was explicit in its decision to denounce Marxism, stating that: "in 1981 the main issue was how to break with capitalism. […] Today everyone talks about modernization" (cited in Sassoon 1996: 559). Greece's Pan-Hellenic Socialist Movement (PASOK) regrouped in the mid-1980s and announced a significant change in its economic policy; while in 1979, when it came into power, the Spanish Socialist Workers Party (PSOE) decided to drop "Marxist maximalism."

In the context of this book's focus on the ideologically similar Greek Coalition of the Radical Left (SYRIZA) and Cypriot Progressive Party of Working People (AKEL), it is interesting to examine PASOK, which has many ideological similarities to the two parties. Although PASOK rose to power preaching anti-imperialistic and anti-EEC slogans, it behaved quite differently once in government (Eleftheriou and Tassis 2013; Spourdalakis 1998). Gradually, the party's anti-imperialist, anti-NATO, and anti-EEC positions and slogans were abandoned. In looking at the tactics that the PASOK leadership used to justify ideological modifications so that the party base would accept them, we note the following: the new rhetoric differentiated between short- and long-term targets (i.e., socialism), relegating long-term goals to an unforeseeable future before totally eliminating them; the party explained that unexpected environmental changes necessitated a readjustment to the "contract" it had "signed" with the people, citing certain developments that required short-term compromise. Silently, without ever stating it, the party abandoned its earlier policies geared towards socialism, nationalizations, and so on until they were totally forgotten (Diamantopoulos 1991: 69–85; Spourdalakis 1988).

Following the dissolution of the socialist bloc, which meant that the party was operating in a more secure political and party environment, at least in terms of opposition from the Left, PASOK gradually mapped out a course of identification with the state (Vernardakis 2011: 13). The party that in the 1970s and 1980s had called for change, in the 1990s became a cartel party (see Katz and Mair 1995, for discussion of this concept). The government was then independent of not only the party but also the parliamentary team, while party organization was totally ignored so that government policies were in no way jeopardized.

The overall scheme charted by South Europe socialist parties—of which PASOK is a very good example—revealed a gradual but linear movement towards the centre. Initially, they radicalized in order to rise electorally, gaining from their more leftist competitors and against the ruling class that excluded them from government. Subsequently, the socialist parties moderated their goals so that they could be included in the inner-party system and be accepted as legitimate governing actors. This led them to emphasize the politics of symbolic competition. "Marxism never provided socialist parties of western Europe with any significant practical counsel in government" (Sassoon 1997: 3–4).

Their "centrist" course continued until they eventually abandoned socialism and adopted social democracy at a time when the social democrats had agreed to social liberalism (see Giddens 1998). Despite the varying degrees to which the parties adhered to social liberalism, they all accepted economic technocratic efficiency over social justice; they considered the Keynesian contract as outdated; they accepted privatizations; and they agreed to the primacy of the markets. Gradually, they also were driven to cartelization.

The Legacy of Eurocommunism

However useful the socialist parties' experience might be, prior to 1990 almost all the RLPs that participated in coalition governments adhered to Eurocommunism, and many of these parties have been criticized for allegedly opening the way to their social democratization (Sodara 1984). It therefore is valuable to review the history of the communist Left's dealings with power and government within the Eurocommunist paradigm.

Eurocommunism was not formulated in a vacuum; it was significantly influenced by world events and developments. These included the following: the situation in Chile with the popular front that brought Allende to government and the subsequent military coup d'état that overturned him, the outcome of the May 1968 revolts in Europe that brought a number of new social movements and actors to the foreground, the Soviet intervention in Czechoslovakia in 1968, and the leftist turn of social democracy in South Europe as a result of the dictatorships in that part of the continent (i.e., Portugal, Spain, and Greece). At the same time, the post-WWII European social model (i.e., the welfare state) led to enormous improvements in working and living conditions for the majority of the people, which resulted in the de-politicization and de-radicalization of the working class (Wahl 2010: 88–89). All these events and developments led a number of western communist parties to question USSR's supremacy and ideological orthodoxy and to seek alternative paradigms.

During the early 1970s and after the Soviet Union's intervention in Czechoslovakia in 1968, the western communist movement systematized the "democratic road to power" theory within the paradigm of Eurocommunism—that is, a strategy for claiming power within capitalism. Among the fundamental premises of Eurocommunism were the following stipulations noted by Balabanidis (2015a) and Dunphy (2004: 24–26):

- A gradual weaning of the communist parties from Moscow, believing that the communist movement had long ago entered a phase of polycentrism.
- Each country would develop its own road to socialism.
- Socialism would be achieved through elections, not revolution, thus embracing liberal democratic institutions.
- Multipartyism was acceptable.
- Criticism of the lack of political freedoms in the USSR.
- Gradual acceptance of the European integration project, albeit in a different direction and context.
- Acceptance of government responsibility.

This was essentially a vision for socialism that claimed to offer a "Third Way" between Stalinism and social democracy. Central to the Eurocommunist parties' theorization was the relationship between the reform communists and the new social movements (e.g., ecology, feminism, anti-nuclear, pacifist, etc.). Accordingly, the new historic bloc[1] would involve the union of working class with these new movements.

The seminal work about this tendency was done by Santiago Carillo (1977), *Eurocommunism and the State*, then the Secretary General of the Communist Party of Spain (PCE). Carillo was heavily influenced by Bernstein (1899, revised 1996) and Kautksy (1985); these authors argued in favour of a nonviolent path to socialism by means of social reforms and political democratization that would lead to a change towards socialism. Carillo took their ideas and further argued that western communist parties could not repeat Lenin's strategy of an armed revolution in the context of advanced Western democracies.

As part of this new strategy, the PCE accepted the restoration of a liberal democracy and constitutional monarchy following the decades-long reign of Franco, which many party members viewed as treason. Carillo's reforms and the social democratization of the party under his leadership provoked dissent among party ranks that eventually led to Carillo's removal from leadership and in 1985 his eventual expulsion (see Sassoon 1996: 616–626, for a discussion about the PCE).

The Italian version of Eurocommunism drew heavily on Gramsci's theory of hegemony (see Ingrao 1979; Grouppi 1977). The most prominent representative was Enrico Berlinguer, Secretary General of the Italian Communist Party (PCI) at the time, and his seminal work, *Historical Compromise* (1977). Gramsci's work, although ambivalent on some aspects, clearly distinguished between political society and civil society. He argued that the state is part of the political society and is characterized by coercion and domination, whereas civil society's main feature is hegemony. Gramsci realized that in Western states bourgeois power spread in multiple lines throughout civil society (differentiating them from Russia), including alternative governing solutions, many parties representing various social interests, mechanisms of ideological hegemony (e.g., the Church), the press, the education system, and so forth.

Gramsci then reasoned that the working class would first exercise hegemony in the civil society realm; this would lead, through elections, to the total seizure of the state. He also theorized the concept of the "war of positions," which refers to a gradual undermining of the bourgeois state, and the "war of movements," which promotes a more aggressive strategy towards power acquisition. The Eurocommunist ideology, espouses primarily the *war of positions*, which justifies government participation as part of the Left's penetration into state institutions in order to question and then weaken mainstream ideologies and practices that cement the bourgeois domination. In this respect, even bourgeois institutions can be mobilized for novel social purposes because their outcomes and practices are dependent on and shaped by social and political conflict (Bruff 2014: 116).

Based on this theorization, the PCI developed its "Historic Compromise" project during the 1970s (Sassoon 1996: 572–593; Ingrao 1983). Amid a very turbulent social and political period in Italy, sparked by an economic crisis and marked by strikes and increased social unrest, Berlinguer claimed that a greater social majority was needed in order to safeguard Italy's constitutional order. This majority would consist of the Communists, the Socialists, and the Christian Democrats. According to the PCI, this was the only road to power for the party because, despite its differentiation from Moscow, it was excluded permanently from the inner-party system. Therefore, the only way to acquire legitimacy and to be considered as a legitimate governing partner was to be accepted as such by the principal systemic party—the Christian Democrats.

Following the PCI's participation in government a peculiar, at the time, theory of communist modernization emerged that included the acceptance of austerity measures. The PCI argued that it would benefit the working class if Italy exited the crisis before pursuing any other social target (i.e., socialism), because there would be more jobs and time to plan the country's economic activity. Accordingly, the PCI said it was imperative that a clash between capital and labour be avoided while the economic crisis persisted. The party's goal during that specific period was not socialism but was to save the national economy and this required sacrifices on behalf of the working class.

Greece's Eurocommunism was shaped decisively by the prominent Greek intellectual Nicos Poulantzas in his famous work, *The State, Power, Socialism* (1978). He was influenced by the May 1968 worker/student revolts that resulted in the emergence of new social movements (Kriesi et al. 1995; Inglehart 1977). Poulantzas argued for a more leftist direction than the respective Italian and Spanish (and the French) communist parties and called for a more movement-oriented strategy. Poulantzas believed that the masses would not accept revolutionary conditions for a long time, and he also was concerned about the (un)willingness of people to take mass action given the fact that they lived in conditions of passive representative democracy (Mpelantis 2014: 90).

Poulantzas argued that the Left should take these concerns into account and plan the gradual and departmental takeover of the state. However, he highlighted the significance of questioning state mechanisms and their configuration, and he looked closely at the party's relationship to grassroots movements, arguing that if these issues were ignored the Left ran the risk of identifying with classic social democracy. Poulantzas believed that the process of capturing power would also be a process of state transformation through popular struggles (1978: 141). As Poulantzas envisioned things, the state would be a locus of struggle but not the only one (Brie 2010: 30). Poulantzas's democratic road to socialism was based on successive small battles that would enable the communist parties to acquire better positions both within and outside state mechanisms. The Greek reformist communist party, the Communist Party of the Interior (KKE-*Es*, forerunner of Synaspismos), espoused the ideas of Poulantzas; however, it was never in a position to claim government participation during the 1970s and 1980s. Being too small electorally and continuously introverted, it was unable to present any real threat to the KKE and the socialists (PASOK).

The ideological shift of the communist parties in South Europe in the pre-1990 period facilitated joint ventures with socialists and social democrats that attempted to come together on the basis of various joint governing projects: the "joint programme" in France (1974–1978), the "historic compromise" in Italy (1976–1979), and the "forces of change" in Greece (1981) (Sassoon 1996: 534–644). These programmes promoted the creation and/or enhancement of the welfare state, the democratization of the state, and the inclusion of Left forces in governing coalitions. The new era that dawned after the 1989 breakup of the Soviet bloc meant that communist or socialist ventures would be pursued in a very different social and political international setting.

THE FALL OF THE USSR

The collapse of the socialist bloc posed a serious identity crisis for communist parties worldwide (Bosco 2001: 329); it not only deprived them of a concrete example to validate their socialist vision, but it also reinforced the general belief that capitalism and the forces of the free market were the only options. As early as 1992, Fukuyama (1992) pointed to the "end of history," suggesting that democratic capitalism was the final stop in human development. His thesis was increasingly accepted by many social democratic and socialist parties, as well as by a significant number of reform communist and former communist parties. There was a sense that even the most democratic Left project was somehow buried in the ruins of the Berlin wall.

At the same time neo-liberalism, which had begun to make waves during the early 1980s (Panitch 1986), now took centre stage, leading to the overturn of Keynesian economics throughout the advanced world and dominating politics. Deprived of any organized ideological counterweight, capitalism was liberated from all the constraints that had been placed on it: nationalization, progressive taxation, workers' rights, social security regulation, and so on. Globalization began to be promoted intensively as a means of opening up the markets, and all protectionist measures against the free flow of capital were abolished; meanwhile, the working class, once the central electoral pillar of communist parties, became extremely fragmented. These developments silenced any discussion among the communist and radical Left parties about government participation and the claiming of power. New issues, such as criticism of neo-liberalism and of globalization, the fight against imperialist wars, nationalism, and racism, were prioritized in their agendas.

The various communist parties reacted differently to the dissolution of the socialist regimes (see March 2008: 5; March and Mudde 2005: 27; Bell 1993: 10–11); their responses were informed largely by domestic communist traditions. Those communist parties that dissociated early from Moscow's foreign policy and adopted a reformist, Eurocommunist identity (e.g., the Nordic parties) found it easier to adopt a post-Communist identity and to survive the USSR's collapse unscathed, albeit totally transformed. Nevertheless, several countries with a strong radical tradition continued to maintain a stable communist party into the 1990s and some (e.g., Cyprus, Greece, Portugal, France) even beyond then. All communist parties, however, felt the weight of their ideological baggage at this critical juncture, in one sense or another, and all experienced internal tensions (Bull and Heywood 1994).

The parties that stood firm in their socialist principles suffered a huge decline in their membership and electoral influence to the degree that their very survival was under threat (Katz and Mair 1992: 335). Overall, since 1989, many western European RLPs appear to have become electorally weakened (Table 2.1); however, in some countries (e.g., Portugal, Cyprus, Greece, the Netherlands, Norway, Germany) the RPLs strengthened their electoral presence during the period 2000–2015 compared to the previous decade (1990–1999).

The majority of the communist parties underwent profound change. The way in which they changed also was influenced by their internal balance of power. Like the Green parties in the 1980s (see Kitschelt 1988), communist (and radical Left) parties are divided into *Realos* and *Fundis*;

Table 2.1 Average electoral strength of the RLPs in Western Europe (1980–2015)

Decades/country	1980s	1990s	2000s	2010–2015
Denmark	12.6	7.7	8.5	9.2
Sweden	5.6	7.6	7.2	5.7
Finland	13.5	10.7	9.4	8.1
Spain	6.4	10.8	4.8	6.9
Portugal	15.9	10.7	13.8	13.1
Cyprus	30.1	31.8	32.9	32.7
Greece	12	10.9	11.9	37
France	14.2	9.6	7.4	6.9
Netherlands	–	2.4	9.6	9.8
Norway	6.8	7	9.2	4.1
Germany	–	4	8.2	8.6
Italy	–	6.7	6.5	5.7
Luxemburg	5.1	2.5	3.3	4.9
Average % per decade	**12.3**	**9.4**	**10.2**	**11.7**

Source: Spyropoulou (2015): 54

this division also occurs internally. If the Realos were dominant, the parties moved towards classic social democracy or Left libertarianism. Whenever the Fundis were stronger, important ideological associations with their past remained. However, also like the Greens, the Realos gradually became dominant in most RLP leaderships (March 2008: 10).

The year 1989 represented a turning point for Eurocommunist parties; ever since that time these parties have shown an increasing reconciliation with liberal democracy, focusing on broadening its limits and making it even more democratic. As a result, almost overnight, the once powerful South Europe communist parties became democratic socialists or Left democrats. For example, the Italian PCI abandoned its communist past and was renamed the Democratic Party of the Left, aligning with the Socialist International. As the then party leader, A. Ochetto, explained: "the party had long been a party of democratic socialism but the name and its symbols prevented the wider public from voting for the party" (see Sassoon 1996: 752). Essentially, the PCI harmonized its practice with its theory, as did most reformist communist parties.

To remain relevant many of those then-transformed RLPs turned to government participation; since the early 1990s, parties to the left of social democracy have participated in governments in Finland, Norway, Iceland, France, Italy, Ireland, Cyprus, and most recently in Greece. Their successes and failures, including their own analyses of the experience, have been hotly debated not only inside the parties but also by other RLPs that are nearing government participation (e.g., see Daiber 2010).

The Fundamental Issues and the Divergent Strategies

Probably the most important question plaguing the modern radical Left is whether a class-based Left is politically "allowed" to take part in a government coalition or whether it can even accept this role if it means subscribing to a Left government programme that promotes the classic social democratic paradigm. Would taking a road where they can effect some reforms and small changes be enough to promote the socialist target and democratize the state, or would such a path only lead to the Left parties being incorporated within the system they want to change (Miliband 1978: 168–69)? Some argue that this must not only be allowed but that it also must be pursued (Spourdalakis 2013; Brie 2010).

This strategy combines, at least theoretically, activist and social movement characteristics with left-wing governmentalism. The implicit assumption of this strategy is change from within. The argument is that the Left taking part in government coalitions, or even governing on their own within capitalism, is a necessary step in the process of transforming the state and society—governing in this way is the vehicle of change. As globalization and European integration advance, however, and in order to be successful, the parties must form broad societal and political alliances outside their countries (e.g., within the EU context), thus Europeanizing their demands (Daiber and Kulke 2010: 7–8).

The danger in this strategy is that the Left could become reduced to pursuing humanizing capitalism as the ultimate goal. This would make the governing Left responsible for integrating itself into a capitalist and liberal democratic model (Panayotakis 2010: 21; Weber 1987; Althusser 1980). When the RLPs assimilate with the state, they tend to prioritize citizens' everyday problems over any other goal, which eventually leads to de-radicalization. Radicalization typically results from extraparliamentary struggle, whereas elections constitute a mechanism of de-radicalization that necessitates moderation in order to win over undecided and centrist voters (Weber 1987).

A crucial aspect in this conundrum is the role of the government vis-à-vis the governing party. Will the party submit to the needs of governing or will it continue to champion extraparliamentary social causes? Will it maintain its autonomous role or will it become a branch of the government? Clearly, if the party is involved in government, the party itself is a crucial variable. It is important for the party to have the ability to effectively and comprehensively analyze the situation and the surrounding environment, as well as to have a strategy to implement at least some degree of social change. This strategy should be a part of a larger plan for bringing about social transformation (Wahl 2010: 90–92). The latter, as evidence suggests, has not been well developed by the RLPs.

Communist parties in the past usually have resolved this issue by dividing the party programme in two: a minimum and a maximum program. Radical Left parties tend to mimic this tactic. A *minimum* program refers to immediate claims, mainly democratic and economic, whereas a *maximum* program refers to the party's strategic goals of socialism and achieving political power for the working class. Generally, strategic goals are treated as matters of ideology because the Left feels that present conditions are not right for pursuing their agenda. This strategy includes the danger of transforming the party into a permanent electoral machine. Another tactical approach related to governing is to offer critical support to centre-left governments, as this would allow room for movement and the chance to pursue primary positions and more radical proposals than the often watered-down compromises needed in government (Wahl 2010: 94).

An alternative strategy is the one proposed by Holloway (2006): a decision to not partake in governing coalitions but to remain outside the bourgeois power system, choosing instead to create institutions and forms of social organizations free of capitalist domination as a model for the future society they envisage. This position derives partially from the Luxemburg (1900) thesis that capitalism cannot be changed but only abolished, which will be accomplished through revolution because the state, she says, is nothing more than the instrument of the economic ruling elite. In Holloway's view then, government participation not only weakens the Left but also essentially nullifies it.

This strategy is similar to that of the Zapatistas in Mexico during the mid-1990s. The Zapatistas worked towards the progressive substitution of capitalism, utilizing various forms and schemes of collectives, social laboratories, and communes. The strategy has as its aim not to conquer power but to block it from penetrating the social spaces, then to deny it, and finally to arrest it completely. The danger inherent in this strategy is that creating many small oases within the capitalist desert means that in their isolation they very easily could be destroyed.

Once the RLPs join (coalition) governments further questions arise (Olsen et al. 2010: 3, 5): Do these parties perform as well in government as they do in opposition? Are RLPs ready to practice politics as the "art of the possible" and adjust their policies to the difficult business of governing, despite inevitable claims of ideological betrayal by some of their members? Or, on the contrary, do they promise much and deliver very little when they are given the opportunity to take part in national governments? Their challenge is to continue to articulate a distinct political vision and a set of clear policy principles; at the same time, they must be able to compromise these principles to the degree that they can actually implement their policies.

Their biggest challenge is to combine idealism with factual policy proposals. As Dunphy and Bale (2011: 490) point out: "ideology still has an important role to play for the radical Left." Arguably, the RLPs' most prominent stake is to maintain their radical identity in the process of striving for and achieving office. To address these questions generalities and incomplete theorizations are inadequate. Therefore, the next chapters offer a detailed analysis that delves deeply into the specific conditions of each party and country under study here, and their histories and traditions, and they look at the balance of power between political forces.

NOTE

1. A historic bloc is a concept coined by A. Gramsci in his *Prison Notebooks*. According to him a historical bloc refers to "a historical congruence between material forces, institutions and ideologies, or broadly, an alliance of different class forces politically organized around a set of hegemonic ideas that give strategic directions and coherence to its constituent elements."

BIBLIOGRAPHY

Althusser L. (1980). *On the Crisis of Marxism*, Athens: Agonas [in Greek].

Balabanidis, Y. (2015a). 'Radical Left, the Heir of Many Ancestors', *Sygxrona Themata*, 130–131 (December), pp. 46–50 [in Greek].

Bell, D.S., (Ed.) (1993). *Western European Communists and the Collapse of Communism*, Oxford, UK: Berg Publishers.

Berlinguer, E. (1977). *Historical Compromise*, Athens: Themelio [in Greek].

Bernstein, D. [1899] (1996). *The Preconditions of Socialism and the Duties of Social Democracy*, Athens: Papazisis [in Greek].

Bosco, A. (2001). 'Four Actors in Search of a Role: The Southern European Communist Parties', in N. Diamandouros and R. Gunther (Eds), *Parties, Politics and Democracy in the New Europe*, Baltimore: John Hopkins University Press.

Brie, M. (2010). 'Is Socialist Politics Possible in Government? Five Objections by Rosa Luxemburg and Five Offers for a Discussion', in Daiber, B. (Eds.) *The Left in Government. Latin America and Europe Compared*, Brussels: Rosa Luxemburg Foundation, pp. 21–34.

Bruff, I. (2014). 'The Rise of Authoritarian Neoliberalism', *Rethinking Marxism*, 26(1), pp. 113–129.

Bull, M.J. and Heywood, P. (Eds). (1994). *West European Communist Parties after the Revolutions of 1989*, Basingstoke: Macmillan.

Carillo, S. (1977). *Eurocommunism and the State*, Athens: Themelio [in Greek].

Daiber, B. (Eds.) *The Left in Government. Latin America and Europe Compared*, Brussels: Rosa Luxemburg Foundation.

Daiber, B. and Kulke, R. (2010). 'Introduction', in Daiber, B. (Eds.) *The Left in Government. Latin America and Europe Compared*, Brussels: Rosa Luxemburg Foundation, pp. 7–20.

Diamantopoulos. T. (1991). *Party Families*, Athens: Exantas [in Greek].

Dunphy, R. (2004). *Contesting Capitalism – Left Parties and European Integration*, Manchester: Manchester University Press.

Dunphy, R. and Bale, T. (2011). 'The radical left in coalition government: Towards a comparative measurement of success and failure', *Party Politics*, 17(4), pp. 488–504.

Eleftheriou, C. and Tassis, Ch. (2013). *PASOK: The Rise and Fall of a Hegemonic Party*, Athens: Savallas [in Greek].

Fukuyama, F. (1992). *The End of History and the Last Man*, New York: Free Press.

Giddens, A. (1998). *The Third Way: The Renewal of Social Democracy*, London: Polity Press.

Grouppi, L. (1977). *The Concept of Hegemony in Gramsci*, Athens: Themelio [in Greek].

Holloway, J (2006). *Change the World without Taking Power*, Athens: Savvalas [in Greek].

Inglehart, R. (1977). *The Silent Revolution: Changing Values and Political Styles among Western Publics*, Princeton: Princeton University Press.

Ingrao, P. (1983). *The Crisis and the Third Way*, Athens: Politipo.

Ingrao, P. (1979). *The Masses and Power*. Athens: Themelio.

Ilada, I. (2010). 'The Left in Government, the Crisis of Capitalism and Post-Neoliberalism: Challenges and Political Perspectives for the Implementation of a New Model of Socio-Economic Development in Brazil', in Daiber, B. (Eds.) *The Left in Government. Latin America and Europe Compared*, Brussels: Rosa Luxemburg Foundation, pp. 75–84.

Kautksy, K. (1985). *The Social Revolution*, Athens: Papazisis [in Greek].

Katz, R., and Mair, P. (1995). 'Changing Models of Party Organization: the Emergence of the Cartel Party', *Party Politics*, 1 (1), pp. 5–28.

Katz, R., and Mair, P., (1992). 'The Membership of Political Parties in European Democracies, 1960–90'. *European Journal of Political Research*, 22(3), pp. 329–345.

Kitschelt H. (1988). 'Left-libertarian Parties: Explaining Innovation in Competitive Party Systems', *World Politics*, XL, pp. 194–234.

Kriesi, H., Koopmans, R., Duyvendak, J. W., and Giugni, M. (1995). *New Social Movements in Western Europe*, Minneapolis/London: University of Minnesota Press/UCL Press.

Luxemburg, R. (1900). *Reform or Revolution*, https://www.marxists.org/archive/luxemburg/1900/reform-revolution/, Accessed 12 September 2015.

March, L. (2011). *Radical Left Parties in Europe*, London: Routledge.

March, L. (2008). Contemporary Far Left Parties in Europe – From Marxism to the Mainstream? Friedrich Ebert Foundation, November 2008, Berlin: library. fes.de/pdf-files/id/ipa/05818.pdf.

March. L., and Mudde, C. (2005). 'What's left of the radical left? The European Radical Left after 1989: Decline and Mutation', *Comparative European Politics*, 3 (1), pp. 23–49.

Miliband, R. (1978). 'Constitutionalism and Revolution: Notes on Eurocommunism', *The Socialist Register*, I(xvi), pp. 158–171.
Mouzelis, N. (1994). *Nationalism and Late Development*. Athens: Themelio [in Greek].
Mpelantis, D. (2014). *The Left and Power: The "Democratic Way" to Socialism*, Athens: Topos [in Greek].
Olsen, J., Koß, M., and Hough, D. (2010). 'From Pariahs to Players? Left parties in National Governments. In J. Olsen, M. Koß and D. Hough (eds.) *Left Parties in Government*, New York: Palgrave Macmillan, pp. 1–15.
Panayotakis, C. (2010). 'Capitalism, Socialism, and Economic Democracy: Reflections on Today's Crisis and Tomorrow's Possibilities', *Capitalism Nature Socialism*, 21(4), pp. 7–33.
Panitch, L. (1986). *Working Class Politics in Crisis*, London: Verso.
Pinto, A. C. and Teixeira, N. S. (2002) (Eds). *Southern Europe and the Making of the European Union*, New York: Columbia University Press.
Poulantzas, N. (1978). *The State, Power, Socialism*, London: New Left Review Editions.
Przeworski, A. (1980). 'Social Democracy as a Historical Phenomenon', *New Left Review*, I/122, pp. 27–58.
Sassoon, D. (Ed) (1997). *Looking Left*, London: I. B. Tauris.
Sassoon, D. (1996). *One Hundred Years of Socialism: The West European Left in the Twentieth Century*, London: I. B. Tauris.
Smith, W. R. (2015), *Enemy Brothers: Socialists and Communists in France, Italy and Spain*, London: Rowman and Littlefield.
Sodara, M. J., (1984). 'Whatever Happened to Eurocommunism', *Problems of Communism*, November-December, pp. 59–65.
Spourdalakis, M. (2013), 'Left Strategy in the Greek Cauldron: Explaining SYRIZA's Success', in L. Panitch, G. Albo and V. Chibber (Eds), *Socialist Register 2013: The Question of Strategy*, London: Merlin Press, pp. 98–120.
Spourdalakis, M. (Eds) (1998). *PASOK. Party – State - Society*. Athens: Patakis [in Greek].
Spourdalakis, M. (1988), *The Rise of the Greek Socialist Party*, London: Routledge.
Spyropoulou, V. (2015). 'The European Radical Left: Electoral Development 1990-2015', *Sygxrona Themata*, Issue 130–131, December, pp. 51–60 [in Greek].
Vernardakis, C. (2011). *Political Parties, Elections and the Party System: The Transformations of Political Representation 1990-2010*, Athens: Sakkoulas [in Greek].
Wahl, A. (2010). 'To be in Office, but not in Power: Left Parties in the Squeeze between Peoples' Expectations and an Unfavourable Balance of Power', in Daiber, B. (Eds.) *The Left in Government. Latin America and Europe Compared*, Brussels: Rosa Luxemburg Foundation, pp. 85–94.
Weber, H. (1987). 'Tactic and Strategy of the Left in western Europe', *Theseis*, 18, pp. 19–48 [in Greek].

CHAPTER 3

SYRIZA: The History of the Struggle of Factions

Abstract SYRIZA's rise from the margins of the Greek political system to prominence in a very short period of three years necessitates the study of the party's historical path. This examination also must include its ideological and organizational traditions in order to arrive at a holistic understanding. The party is placed in context here by looking at how it developed on three interrelated levels: the wider party system after 1974, the Greek Left bloc, and the party itself.

Keywords Greek Left • Synaspismos • PASOK • SYRIZA • Organization • Ideology • Metapolitefsi • Elections

The Greek Left historically has been marked by introversion and fragmentation (Lyrintzis 2011: 18), with the Communist Party of Greece (KKE) consistently being the dominant intrabloc party. The other Left parties included many with Marxist leanings as well as several with revolutionary and extremist left tendencies (Marioulas 2010; Kassimeris 2001). The modern Greek Left is mostly made up of the KKE, the Coalition of the Radical Left (SYRIZA), the Democratic Left (DIMAR), the extraparliamentary Anti-capitalist Left Cooperation for the Overthrow

---

This simile was used by Vernardakis (2011: 277) to describe Synaspismos, paraphrasing Marx's well-known thesis: "the history of the world is the history of the struggle between social classes."

© The Editor(s) (if applicable) and The Author(s) 2016
Y. Katsourides, *Radical Left Parties in Government*,
DOI 10.1057/978-1-137-58841-8_3

(Antarsya),[1] and the Popular Unity (LAE)—parties that are ideologically quite disparate. Throughout the post-Cold War era the overall appeal of the Left remained stagnant (Verney 2014; Teperoglou and Tsatsanis 2014); the situation changed almost literally overnight in 2012 when SYRIZA's vote share skyrocketed.

SYRIZA represented, before its founding congress in 2013, a political coalition comprising the democratic socialist party, the Coalition of Left and Progress (Synaspismos), and a number of extraparliamentary Left and left social democratic groups; Synaspismos furnished SYRIZA with most of its political personnel and programmatic goals (Spourdalakis 2013: 102). Throughout its history and until SYRIZA's election to government in January 2015, the party was plagued by heated intraparty discussions and intense relationships with other leftist factions. To understand SYRIZA's rapid rise to power and its political character, we must study the party in relation to the entire Greek Left, including the Panhellenic Socialist Movement (PASOK), as well as in relation to its own past.

THE GREEK LEFT IN HISTORY

The Greek Left has had a very turbulent history. From the margins of times past during the period between the two World Wars, to its absolute heyday in the period of Nazi occupation (1941–1944), to its eventual proscription following the deadly civil war in 1946–1949 (Close 1993; Vernardakis and Mavris 1991), the Greek Left's history has been marked by glorious actions, prosecution by the authorities, intense internal rivalries, exclusions, and marginalization. The Greek Left was always strongly linked to communism; and unlike in western Europe, in Greece there was never any breakup of the labour movement into communists and social democrats until 1974 (Vernardakis and Mavris 1991: 108). This was largely because of the strong KKE, under which the labour movement was united. Nevertheless, the KKE suffered many internal rivalries and schisms; and it was one such schism that led to the founding of KKE-Esoterikou (literally interior), which became Synaspismos (and SYRIZA's predecessor).

Following the party's proscription in the aftermath of the 1946–1949 civil war, in 1951 the KKE formed an umbrella organization, the United Democratic Left (EDA), with a modus operandi that came to resemble that of Synaspismos. The EDA was a mass party incorporating a number of leftist organizations and personalities with the KKE being the dominant partner (see Meynaud 2002: 229–268, for EDA details).

The party's political strategy was characterized by defensive strategies and an emphasis on parliamentarism and loose organizational structures (Vernardakis and Mavris 1991: 107); its political programme was modelled on "National Democratic Change"—a manifesto adopted in 1956 that provided for a peaceful passage to socialism. EDA was dissolved in 1967 following the military coup d'état.

In 1968, the USSR's intervention in Czechoslovakia led the KKE to split into two parties: the KKE and the KKE-*Es*. The KKE was comprised of those cadres and voters who remained loyal to Moscow and who stayed in exile until the country's democratization in 1974 (Clogg 1987: 177); while the KKE-*Es* consisted of party cadres operating illegally inside Greece and adopting Eurocommunism (see Mpenas 2011, and Kapetanyannis 1979, for a review of the KKE-*Es*). After the country's transition to democracy in 1974, the KKE and the KKE-*Es* followed two different political trajectories, respectively, "orthodox" and Eurocommunist (Kalyvas and Marantzides 2002); the former was consistently more successful than the latter in electoral terms (Table 3.1).

The importance of ideology in the KKE-*Es*' party culture caused continuous intraparty tensions that resulted in splits and exits. The first serious schism occurred in 1978 when the party youth organization, EKON-Regas Fereos, left the party en masse and formed a new organization, the "EKON Regas Fereos Second Panelladiki." This latter organization advocated Left Eurocommunism and considered the KKE-*Es* policy too right wing. In 1986 the KKE-*Es* split once again—terminally this time—into the Greek Left (EAR) and the KKE-*Es* Reformist Left. In the 1989 elections the EAR joined the Coalition of Left and Progress (i.e., Synaspismos), which was formed in cooperation with the KKE. This electoral coalition

Table 3.1   KKE-*Es* and KKE electoral results, 1977–1985

Year	Type of elections	Votes		%		Seats	
		KKE-Es	KKE	KKE-Es	KKE	KKE-Es	KKE
1977	National	139.356	480.272	272	936	2	11
1981	European	275.731	729.052	515	1284	1	3
1981	National	76.404	620.302	134	1093	0	13
1984	European	203.813	693.304	342	1164	1	3
1985	National	117.135	629.518	184	989	1	12

Source: Ministry of Interior, Electoral Results of Parliamentary Elections, accessed 29 August 2015

dissolved two years later when the KKE withdrew. Synaspismos was then transformed into a (reformist Left) party and struggled to find its place in the Greek political system for more than two decades as it hovered between the KKE and PASOK.

The Metapolitefsi

The year 1974 was a turning point for the Greek Left as well as for the entire country; after seven years of a harsh military dictatorship, a genuine transition to democracy was inaugurated. This was the start of a new historical era marked by a stable democratic regime, popularly known as the Third Greek Republic or *Metapolitefsi*. The structural transformation of the political system at the time was possible only because the social bases of political representation had changed radically (Kotsaka and Kotsonopoulos 2012). Old allegiances and social hierarchies were shattered, making way for new political alliances and ideologies, which reshaped the political scene.

The political system that fell into place was dominated by antagonism between the two major political parties: *Nea Dimokratia* (New Democracy, ND) and PASOK, representing the centre-right and the centre-left, respectively. The party system was complemented by the communist Left (KKE) as well as by minor parties, all of which failed to thrive except for Synaspismos (Lyrintzis 2011: 3). Greece's desire for stability combined with the country's electoral law meant that the Left parties remained of only marginal importance throughout this period (Verney 2014).

The Metapolitefsi can be divided in three main periods (Vernardakis 2011: xxi–xxii). In the *early Metapolitefsi* (1974–1981) political parties were consolidated and the foundations of political representation were laid. During this period the political parties were the main contours of democratization, which enabled the Left to develop freely either by legalizing the leftist parties or by joining the newly founded PASOK. Before long PASOK was the most important political actor not only within the Left bloc but also in the entire political and party system of Greece (Eleftheriou and Tassis 2013).

Political representation was organized along the model of mass parties with PASOK leading the transition (Spourdalakis 1988). By the 1980s this model was so dominant that the Third Greek Republic had become a "party democracy"—that is, social demands were ideologically expressed and channeled mainly through party representation. This social alignment to party politics was evident because of the widespread party presence, which permeated society from trade unionism to academic politics. During the second phase, or the *interim Metapolitefsi* (1981–1996), the two main parties (i.e., PASOK and ND) alternated in government; they formed competitive and opposing social blocs based on different ideologies, programmes, and social alignments, delineating a context of a polarized bipartisanship. Political parties remained powerful social institutions but gradually became professional bureaucracies disconnected from their constituencies.

Finally, in the *late Metapolitefsi* (1996–2010), the two dominant mainstream parties, PASOK and ND, converged on the ideological construct of modernization (*eksygxronismos*) introduced by PASOK's Prime Minister Costas Simitis in 1996. This signalled PASOK's turn to the right, with the party endorsing an ideology similar to Blair's New Labour. This phase is demarcated by the convergence of the two major parties, both of which took a neo-liberal stance therefore indicating both their cartelization and a type of "consensual bipartisanship"; this, thus, increased the perception among the population that there were no real differences between them (Spourdalakis 2003). The 2010 Memorandum with the Troika seemed to demarcate the end of the Metapolitefsi.

As noted in Chap. 1, the evolution of PASOK offers a very instructive model for South Europe's radical Left parties (RLPs), and especially for the Greek (and Greek Cypriot) parties. In its initial years, the PASOK advocated a third-world type of socialism and Keynesian economics combined with populist practices and radical rhetoric conveyed through a charismatic leader; this mixture led to spectacular growth both organizationally and electorally (Spourdalakis 2013: 101). PASOK's archetypal populism promoted the demands of the "nonprivileged" for social justice, popular sovereignty, and national independence, while it accused the (right-wing) establishment of monopolizing political access and economic privilege, often with the help of external powers (Stavrakakis and Katsambekis 2014: 124). Through this rhetoric PASOK established its long hold on the Greek political culture (Lyrintzis 1987).

As many scholars have emphasized (e.g., Eleftheriou and Tassis 2013; Vernardakis 2011; Spourdalakis 1998), the party that began as a radical anti-imperialistic one gradually shifted toward the centre-right until it was transformed into a Left social democratic organization to attract centrist voters by the time it rose to power in 1981. By 1985 the party adopted a strategy that focused on state administration, which naturally was accompanied by ideological and programmatic changes—remaining in power was no longer the means to an end, it was the end goal. The decision to pursue power overruled the party's political identity and meant a watering down of its radicalism (Kotsaka and Kotsonopoulos 2012), so controversial issues, such as those concerning foreign policy (e.g., NATO and EU membership), were abandoned. Nevertheless, the PASOK continued to appeal to a broad base both nationwide and across social classes. A major reason for PASOK's widespread appeal during the 1980s was the promise and implementation of an exceedingly generous social policy.

In 1996 PASOK leader Simitis became Prime Minister and his modernization thesis became the dominant narrative in Greek politics (Featherstone 2005; Lyrintzis 2005). For PASOK, modernization meant that the socialist–populist paradigm was dropped, while a new policy of pragmatism was ushered in that emphasized technocratic approaches and managerial tactics to accommodate Greece's entry into the Eurozone. The party introduced a new set of values and strategies that led it from social democracy to social liberalism and, eventually, to a full endorsement of neo-liberalism under a virtual state of (economic) emergency after 2010 (Lyrintzis 2011). At the same time, the PASOK became an organic part of a corrupt system (Vernardakis 2011: 17).

Synaspismos: The Forerunner

The year 1989 heralded a tremendous change in world politics, especially important for the world communist movement. It was also a year of great significance for the Greek Left and the repercussions are being felt to this day, although the reasons cannot to be found in Berlin but rather in Athens (Marioulas 2010: 292). At the beginning of that critical year, the pro-Soviet KKE and the Euro-Communist EAR joined to form Synaspismos (Vernardakis 2006: 338–341; Verney 1989). International and national developments were favourable for the two parties' rapprochement because Gorbachev's "perestroika" had allowed a softening of the lines of division, and both parties saw an opportunity to oppose their common enemy within the Left bloc (i.e., PASOK), which was caught in a moment of weakness (Kapetanyannis 1993). The alliance was fragile from the start, yet its effect was visible at the polls; in June 1989, it won 13.1 % in the parliamentary election that did not provide a standalone government.

What followed after the elections in November 1989, which again failed to produce a government, is considered one of the greatest historical errors of the Greek Left. To strip PASOK and Prime Minister A. Papandreou of his immunity and put him on trial for his part in a bank scandal, the conservative ND and Synaspismos formed a transitional coalition government that ruled until new elections were held in April 1990 (Pridham and Verney 1991). Synaspismos's participation in a conservative government caused profound dissatisfaction within the Greek Left and damaged the party's relationship with PASOK for many years (Marioulas 2010: 293).

International developments (i.e., the collapse of the Soviet Union) soon caught up with the Left alliance. At the 13th Congress of the KKE in February 1991, Aleca Papariga was elected General Secretary by a very narrow majority against Yiannis Dragasakis (currently MP of SYRIZA and vice president of the Greek government). The election represented a victory for party hardliners who immediately expelled reformers from the Central Committee and in June 1991 terminated the KKE's participation in Synaspismos (Doukas 1991). Reform-communists and the remaining members of Synaspismos transformed that coalition into a full-fledged party in June of 1992. Almost half of the KKE's central committee and thousands of its members remained in Synaspismos (Spourdalakis 2013: 101).

On the other hand, the situation in the early 1990s with the collapse of the socialist bloc, the advancement of neo-liberalism worldwide, and the reemergence of nationalism (especially in the Balkans, so directly affecting Greece) was not ideal even for a new (reformist) Left party. The success of the venture also was compromised by the very ideologically different motives of the two founding groups: former members of the KKE and former members of EAR—the most reformist faction of the former KKE-Es. The inherently contradictory ideological approaches of the leadership helped to entrench various ideological groups and hindered any chance for further development (Mpalafas 2012: 30, 34). As Dragasakis (2012: 13) himself acknowledged: "Synaspismos had no official ideology and theory and for many years it was defined more by its opposition to what it denounced; i.e., communism and social democracy, than by what it actually stood for."

The very different origin and ideology of these two groups, as well as many others that joined Synaspismos, necessitated the creation of a party resembling a political federation—in the footsteps of EDA—and not a solid party organization. In effect, Synaspismos constituted an umbrella organization for a number of factions, tendencies, movements, and so on, a state of affairs that was eventually institutionalized through the party statute marking all future developments (Papademetriou and Spourdalakis 1994: 144–146). The perpetual conflict between the two main factions had two long-term effects: an ideologically ambiguous political programme, and an agreed-on modus operandi that secured (office) benefits for both factions based on their respective results in intraparty elections (Vernardakis 2011: 277).

A *periodization* of the party along the lines proposed by Vernardakis (2011: 278–290) highlights its important characteristics. The *first phase* covers the period June 1992, when the party was formed, through December 1993, when it failed to secure parliamentary representation in the national elections and its first leader (Maria Damanakis) stepped down (Table 3.2). In its early years Synaspismos was a typical centre-left party with the reformists dominating (i.e., the former EAR); it accepted the Maastricht Treaty and presented the early version of a "progressive modernization" programme for Greece as a basis for a coalition government with PASOK (Synaspismos 1992). During this first period, it was the party's relationship with PASOK that divided the party more than anything else, producing numerous intraparty conflicts (Mpalafas 2012: 23, 37).

The *second phase* began in 1994 with the election of Nicos Constantopoulos (father of Zoe Constantopoulou, former president of the Parliament in SYRIZA's first governing tenure) as party leader and ended in 2004 when Alecos Alavanos took over. This period can be

Table 3.2   Synaspismos's electoral results, 1993–2009

Year	Type of elections	Votes	%	Seats
1993	National	202,887	2.94	0
1994	European	408,072	6.29	2
1996	National	347,236	5.1	10
1999	European	331,928	5.17	2
2000	National	219,880	3.20	6
2004	National	241,714	3.26	6
2004	European	254,447	4.15	1
2007	National	361,101	5.04	14
2009	European	240,898	4.7	1
2009	National	351,627	4.6	13

Source: Ministry of Interior, Electoral Results of Parliamentary Elections, accessed 29 August 2015

further divided in two other periods: 1994–2000 and 2000–2004. The earlier period marked a transitional phase for Synaspismos during which the reformists gradually lost ground to the radical leftists. In 1996, at the second Party Congress, Synaspismos tried to dissociate itself from the Maastricht Treaty on account of its neo-liberalism and denounced any cooperation with PASOK. Moreover, a year later it voted down the Amsterdam Treaty; these were both clear signs of dissociation from its centre-left past. At the party's refusal to pursue cooperation with PASOK, a number of prominent figures and members exited from Synaspismos and in 2000 formed a new organization, the "Renewing Modernizing Movement of the Left" (AEKA), which did work with PASOK (Alexatos 2008: 32).

During the period of 2000–2004, the leftists intensified their fight against the reformists. As Vernardakis (2011: 284) noted: "[I]t was a fight for the soul of the party focusing on opposing ideological perceptions of its role in society." The reformists wanted the party to pursue government participation, while the leftists strongly opposed any cooperation with PASOK and looked for collaboration with the emerging social movements and even with the KKE. Constantopoulos's presidential team sided with the Left Current (*Aristero Revma*) and together they built a leftist-oriented profile aiming "to fight against neo-liberalism" (Synaspismos 2000). Their stance was revealed at the 2003 Programmatic Congress (Synaspismos 2003), signalling a rupture with the party's own past (Dragasakis 2012: 13). The party was renamed the Coalition of the Left, the Movements and Ecology. During this period factionalism was institutionalized (see following section), which Vernardakis (2011: 285) believes was a concession to the remaining reformists to prevent their exit from the party.

The 2004 Left Turn and SYRIZA as an Umbrella Organization

In 2000, at the height of PASOK's modernizing project and on the initiative of Synaspismos, several small leftist extraparliamentary organizations, informal groups, and independent activists formed a network, the Space for Dialogue for the Unity and the Common Action of the Left, to consider cooperation possibilities (Tsakatika and Eleftheriou 2013: 10–11). The group set up an organizational and political framework to unite various Left forces under the guidance of Synaspismos. The first alliance made joint protests against the Kosovo War and the G-8 Summit in Genoa, followed by other instances of joint actions (e.g., the European Social

Forum), and by 2004 had agreed on a common electoral platform. The most important link among these various platforms and organizations was their opposition to neo-liberalism and their joint actions had a significant radicalizing effect on Greek society that Synaspismos was quick to incorporate.

In 2004, with the aim of helping Synaspismos secure the 3 % threshold required for parliamentary representation, the Coalition of the Radical Left was founded. SYRIZA grew out of the previously described organizational network; Synaspismos was key to its success because of its relative size and its strong Left leanings under the leadership of Alecos Alavanos. Alavanos was elected at the 4th Party Congress in 2004 and his tenure (2004–2008) represents the *third phase* in the party's evolution, which sealed the Left turn and paved the way for Alexis Tsipras. The political resolution passed by the 2004 congress (Synaspismos 2004) solidified the break with the party's past and reflected its new approach, both in its stance and ideologically explicit wording. The party decried capitalism, the class-based, neo-liberal policies of the European Union (EU) and the Greek elites, the neo-liberal transformation of PASOK, and much more.

In the 2004 intraparty elections the radical leftists represented approximately 65 % of the party membership and the reformists 35 % (Mpalafas 2012: 262). Alavanos, formerly a member of the KKE, crafted a strategy whereby SYRIZA would be the unifying agent for a broad new Left and a presence so strong that it would no longer feel squeezed between PASOK's conformist governmentalism and the KKE (Spourdalakis 2013: 102). Moreover, Alavanos believed that the PASOK was in the midst of a strategic crisis that could lead to Synaspismos being the main opposition force in the country.

In February 2008, at the 5th Party Congress of Synaspismos, Alavanos surprised the party by stepping down. He proposed A. Tsipras as his successor, although he was to remain leader of SYRIZA (Spourdalakis 2013: 103). Tsipras was elected with a vast majority of 70.5 %, compared to the opposing candidate Kouvelis who polled 28.7 % (Mpalafas 2012: 359). Tsipras's election signalled the further decline of the reformists: their representation fell from 35 % in the 2004 congress to 29 % four years later. Surprisingly, Alavanos began to distance himself from Tsipras, and in 2009, together with other representatives of the radical Left, called for SYRIZA to be made a full-fledged party. Tension ensued between the two leaders and, ultimately, Alavanos was not included on the party ticket for the national elections in 2009. Moreover, in the regional elections of 2010, he stood separately from SYRIZA.

The concurrent existence of Synaspismos and SYRIZA often confused both the general public and the party voters, besides occasionally leading to tension between the various factions and component parts. This situation led to the founding of SYRIZA as an umbrella organization. It had been, prior to its founding congress in 2013, a coalition of a number of parties, social movements, and organizations (Table 3.3). Although these were quite ideologically disparate groups, they shared a number of common goals: to fight against the neo-liberal policies of the two major parties, to further develop and strengthen a united Left by promoting a more active strategy and improving their public communication, and to oppose all imperialistic wars. The 2013 party statute of SYRIZA reflected these beliefs.

SYRIZA largely was disabling Synaspismos with regard to both its political programme and its leadership. Along with Tsipras a new generation of younger cadres emerged who took over from the old guard, prompting a battle of the generations within the party (Vernardakis 2011: 289). As the reformists began to realize how little influence they were able to exercise, in 2010 they decided, led by Kouvelis, to exit the party and create a new one: DIMAR (see Spourdalakis 2013: 104–105, for information about this party).

ORGANIZATION

In relation to the other Greek main parties, SYRIZA's membership was small; at the time of the party's founding in 1992, Synaspismos had 22,791 members, most from the large urban centres of Athens and Thessaloniki (Vernardakis 2011: 293). Former KKE members accounted for approximately 70 %, the EAR about 20 %, and other leftist groups and nonaligned citizens made up the last 10 %. Membership fluctuated in the following years, but it revealed a mainly downward trend, especially during the late 1990s. Many members were disappointed by what they saw as the party's factionalism and excessive introspection (Tsakatika and Eleftheriou 2013: 10) so that in 2004 membership fell to 16,376 and by the 2010 congress it had further decreased to 15,500.

The majority of Synaspismos members and voters (prior to its electoral rise in 2012) came from the well-educated and financially secure middle classes, with heavy representation among public employees (Vernardakis 2011: 295). The party also was overrepresented in academia and among

Table 3.3 SYRIZA's constituent parts (until the 2013 founding congress)[a]

Name	Abbreviation	Ideology	Year of accession to SYRIZA	Self-dissolution	Withdrawal
Active Citizens		Democratic socialism, patriotism	2004		2015
Anti-Capitalist Political Group	APO	Trotskyism, anti-capitalism	2011		2015
Citizens Association RIGAS	RIGAS	Left patriotism	2012	2014	
Coalition of Left, of Movements and Ecology	SYNASPISMOS	Eurocommunism, ecosocialism, feminism	2004	2013	
Communist Organization of Greece	KOE	Maoism, communism	2007		2015
Democratic Social Movement	DIKKI	Socialism, Euroscepticism, left-wing nationalism	2007		2015
Greek Ecosocialists		Eco-socialism, green politics	2008	2013	
Internationalist Workers' Left	DEA	Trotskyism (revolutionary socialism)	2004	2014[b]	2015[b]
Movement for the Unity of Action of the Left	KEDA	Communism, Marxism-Leninism	2004		
New Fighter		Democratic socialism	2012		2015
Radical Left Group ROZA	ROZA	Radical left, feminism	2008	2013	
Radicals		Democratic socialism, patriotism	2011		2015
RED	RED	Trotskyism	2004	2014[b]	2015[b]

(continued)

Table 3.3 (continued)

Name	Abbreviation	Ideology	Year of accession to SYRIZA	Self-dissolution	Withdrawal
Renewing Communist Ecological Left	AKOA	Eurocommunism, green politics	2004	2013	
Union of Democratic Center	EDHK	Centrism, social liberalism	2012		2015
United Front	EKM[c]	Socialism, social democracy	2012	2013	
Xekinima (Starting)		Trotskyism	2008		2011

[a]In 2013 SYRIZA's founding congress took place and thereafter all constituent parts were essentially abolished as constituent parts since SYRIZA was transformed into a unitary party. However, most of them regrouped essentially under two new groups: the Left Platform (minority led by P. Lafazanis) housed the former Left Current, DIKKI, DEA, and so forth. The Left Unity (the majority led by A. Tsipras) accommodated the majority of the former constituent parts: ANASA (Initiative for the Recomposition of the Lef—a new group created in 2010 that included the former Red-Green Network, the AKOA, ROZA, the RED, and some nonaligned leftists), KOE, and EKM

[b]In 2014 the RED and DEA merged and in 2015 they left SYRIZA after the signing of the Memorandum and joined LAE

[c]The EKM was not a constituent part but an electoral ally in the 2012 elections, created to assist PASOK members and cadres to move to SYRIZA

the intelligentsia (Marioulas 2010: 294). On the other hand, the party had little support from the Left's traditional base (i.e., workers in industry and in small businesses) and had the lowest level of support among pensioners and housewives.

The ideological origins of the party's membership cover all varieties of Marxism. Synaspismos (and subsequently SYRIZA) included many activists with a genuine Leninist background (i.e., Stalinist, Maoist, and Trotskyist leanings), broad organizational experience, a militant commitment to the Left cause, and immersed in a political culture that made them both loyal and reliable (Spourdalakis 2013: 108). Nonetheless, the very same commitment to the Left was also a source of many problems, as each group had their own reading of Marx and would not accept a collective, party interpretation. Furthermore, a respectable percentage of its members represented the reformist Left, and although Synaspismos, initially and SYRIZA later, tried throughout the years to capitalize on all these various backgrounds, traditions, and experiences, this was not an easy task and often led to serious disputes.

The various ideological backgrounds of its membership, as well as conscious leadership choices, led to a pluralistic and decentralized party model, a situation that led to a number of novel ideas and practices in intraparty life. These notions included the institutionalization of pluralism of opinion, horizontal communication between political movements, and intraparty referendums, among others. Although these may have been democracy-enhancing practices, they were relegated to behind the scenes in a party plagued by so many warring factions.

From the outset, Synaspismos's basic (unwritten) organizational principle was the proportional representation of its constituent factions (Papademetriou and Spourdalakis 1994: 141). Factionalism was not merely an inherent feature of Synaspismos (and later SYRIZA), it was the vehicle through which all party decisions were made and programmes developed. Factions formed intraparty entities with networks that included newspapers, magazines, clubs, and so on. Synaspismos was essentially many parties in one.

As explained earlier, within Synaspismos there was a basic split between two opposing tendencies, a left-wing favouring a critical Europeanism and a more right-wing pursuing government participation in coalition with PASOK (Mpelantis 2014: 214–216; Vernardakis 2011: 276–277). Until the formation of SYRIZA, however, four major factions actually existed (Vernardakis 2011: 281). These factions clashed on various issues,

generally those concerning social and political alliances, the party programme and its character, and party electoral candidates. In addition,
although ideology was a powerful factor, some believed personal motives
(e.g., party control) also featured in the clashes (Mpalafas 2012: 42–43).

The *Syspeirosi* (literally Coiling) faction had existed since the first party
congress in 1992 and was formed by cadres of the former EAR. This was
a centre-left group that advocated convergence and cooperation with
PASOK, so unsurprisingly with the passage of time, many members left
to join PASOK. The *Ananeotiki Protovoulia* (Renewing Initiative) agreed
with *Syspeirosi* on Europeanism and pursuit of a joint coalition programme
with like-minded political forces (i.e., PASOK modernizers) but was more
critical of PASOK. *Paremvasi* (Intervention) brought together some former cadres from the reformist EAR and some ex-KKE members to oppose
the centre-left ideological orientation of the former two factions and tried
to create a more moderate, centrist party.

The more radical leftist faction of *Aristero Revma* (Left Current) tried
for an alliance with the KKE; however, the communists steadfastly rejected
them, claiming that Synaspismos was not a genuine Left party but merely
another branch of social democracy. By early 2010, more than 60 % of
Synaspismos members, including Tsipras, aligned with the Left Current
and 30 % aligned with the Renewal Wing (Marioulas 2010: 301).

The de facto institutionalization of factions occurred in the mid-2000s.
In April 2005 an organizational congress was convened with the purpose
of bringing the statute of the party in line with the new social conditions (i.e., basically the emerging social movements). The congress officially recognized the various factions/tendencies within the party not as
a stream of ideas but as distinct, political groups with their own autonomous procedures and positions (Synaspismos 2005, article 18[6]). Even
though this act essentially brought the statute of the party in line with
reality, it also was seen as recognizing that the party could not be a unitary
party (Vernardakis 2011: 290).

Following SYRIZA's founding congress in 2013 when the tendencies
of Synaspismos ceased to exist, the party again consolidated around two
poles: leftist and centrist. The Left Platform, which grew from the Left
Current, promoted issues such as anti-capitalism and exiting from use of
the euro. The group included a number of organizations and nonaligned
leftists, with Panayiotis Lafazanis as leader. The more centrist faction represented the majority of its then-current leadership headed by Tsipras
himself, and it advocated an institutional, European approach; was against

an exit from the Eurozone; and supported alliances with other Left social and political forces in Europe. They also believed that a "hard" stance toward the EU would harm the party's prospects of governing.

Linkage with Society

The way in which SYRIZA's factions operated and its heavily middle-class membership seem responsible for the party's weak organization; this was evident in its affiliated organizations and therefore its linkage with society. Synaspismos first, and SYRIZA later, was heavily influenced by the tradition of the Italian Left, which highlighted the principles of mutuality and autonomy; thus, the party saw the political Left's role to be "not to guide but to participate in movements and try to influence them, while learning from them" (Tsakatika and Eleftheriou 2013: 11). This, of course, deviated from the classic communist linkage practice that saw the party as the leader of other social movements and organizations (Hayward 1980: 5–6).

Both PASOK and the KKE had stronger ties with the trade unions. That Synaspismos had no comparable union organization was not surprising—we need only look to its social base of support. The Synaspismos-affiliated union, Autonomous Intervention, was always less influential than the KKE and PASOK unions. In 2014 SYRIZA founded a new trade union, the Militant Workers/Employees Class Overturning (META), but again without significant intervention (Eleftheriou 2015). The other organizations affiliated with Synaspismos were analogous to those of other parties: the Nicos Poulantzas Research Institute and the Synaspismos Youth Organization. The party press, *Avgi* (Dawn), was among the smaller of the numerous Greek daily newspapers (Marioulas 2010: 297). In 2006 the party acquired its own radio station, "On the Red."

The Synaspismos Youth Organization, the union of Leftist Youth, was initially very small, with its membership confined to the Athens-based universities—a stark deviation from traditional communist youth organizations (Vernardakis 2011: 295). In 1999 with A. Tsipras its first leader, it began to come into its own through reorganization and involvement in the anti-globalization movement. However, it was not until the later 2000s that it became a union of substance because of its fight against the privatization of higher education in Greece and its involvement in the riots that followed the killing of a 16-year-old student in Athens by the police. During the 2000s, the Synaspismos Youth group became the key intermediary between the party and the social movements (Tsakatika and Eleftheriou 2013: 11).

IDEOLOGY AND PROGRAMME

Political programmes, policies, and proposals generally derive from a specific ideology. This has been especially true for the Left in general and the radical Left in particular. SYRIZA has debated numerous political theories and various "Marxisms," with no ideological tendency dominant within the party. Nonetheless, it is evident that the works of Luxemburg, Gramsci, Poulantzas, and, more recently, those of Hardt and Negri are widely respected (Marioulas 2010: 299). Unlike the "orthodox" communist parties, however, SYRIZA has never drawn much on Lenin.

Synaspismos and SYRIZA engaged heavily in theoretical debates, not only internally, organized numerous public events (e.g., conferences, symposia) and debates focused on theoretical issues pertaining the world's Left movement. Topics included, for example, the Left and Europe, globalization, reforms and the Left, the Left and its theory, the Left and democracy, among many more (Mpalafas 2012: 218). These issues were even discussed in the party press (*Avghi*), in contrast to the orthodox communist parties' practice of internal indoctrination (see Chap. 4 on AKEL). Synaspismos also held programmatic conferences, a largely social democratic practice, to discuss and reach decisions in consultation with its members.

Even the party name, Synaspismos (coalition), is indicative of its ideology, as the party sees itself as representing a broad spectrum of the modern Left. Mirroring its various ideological traditions, Synaspismos defined itself as a pluralist Left party of democratic socialism, neither orthodox communist nor social democratic—a party advocating a mixed economy and placing a fresh emphasis on "new issues," particularly feminism, democratic rights, and the environment (Kalyvas and Marantzidis 2002). The party's founding documents appealed to "the men and women of work and culture, the young and the excluded." This was explicitly not a class appeal because Synaspismos effectively had presented itself as a catch-all party throughout the 1990s.

The party worked during the 1990s to find its place somewhere between communism and social democracy. At first Synaspismos leaned towards social democracy, as evidenced in the party thesis for "progressive modernization." This thesis included the basic premises of Simitis's campaign a few years later—that is, the need to end the state's clientelistic practices that led to serious social and economic deficiencies and malfunctioning, the need to eradicate the flourishing black economy that deprived the state of significant revenues, the need to reorganize the state's infrastructures, the need to strengthen and encourage private initiatives, the promotion of technocratic approaches and the obsoleteness of ideological divides, and so on.

Key to the modernization thesis were the project of European integration and the Maastricht Treaty; the latter, in particular, was seen as a compromise between progressive and conservative European political forces. Thus, the party's acceptance of the Treaty was based on its belief that a struggle from within was required in order to move society/Europe in a leftist, progressive direction. The party's belief that bourgeois institutions could change with the right alliances and specific proposals and that the party should pursue governing as a fundamental function with no references to social transformation indicated that in these early years Synaspismos was closer to social democracy than reform communism (Vernardakis 2011: 280).

Synaspismos differed from popular public opinion, especially during the 1990s, on a number of key issues that were largely included in the "new politics" agenda: separation of church and state, the secular baptisms and funerals, homosexual marriage, the status of immigrants, the rejection of security cameras in public places, the decriminalization of soft drugs, and the position on the conflict over the name of the former Yugoslav Republic of Macedonia. Particularly on those issues considered as "national," the party had a reputation for reticence, which had a negative effect on voters' behaviour. On the other hand, the party was the only one that carried these issues into the parliament (Marioulas 2010: 298).

The party actively sponsored initiatives ranging from public dialogues to demonstrations to promote these as well as other issues such as the improvement of quality of life; the fight against armaments and wars, against nationalism, and against police brutality; the protection of human rights; a stance against racism, among others (Mpalafas 2012: 106). One aspect of the party's ideology that continues to work favourably for SYRIZA was placing ecology and the protection of the environment high on the party's agenda. The importance of this was reflected by the decision to include the term *ecology* into its title in 2001 and in its cooperation with a variety of ecological movements in various elections on joint tickets.

Integral to the party's ideological rhetoric was its insistence on preserving and protecting the democratic and individual rights of all citizens and the democratization of society. Although positively perceived by many human rights activists and Left extraparliamentary organizations, this position led to heavy criticism of Synaspismos, especially after the 9/11 terrorist attacks in the USA, for indirectly harbouring terrorism and providing political shelter to anarchists. Criticism was further heightened in 2002 when the Greek police managed to dismantle the most notorious Greek terrorist organization—the extreme leftist 17N—that was responsible for numerous assassinations and bombings (see Kassimeris 2015: 50–109, for details about 17N). Synaspismos, and SYRIZA later, condemned terrorism but reiterated the importance of protecting the human rights of all citizens.

Reflecting the changes in intraparty factional dynamics with the radical protest-oriented Left Current faction displacing the more moderate Renewal Wing after 2000, Synaspismos policies changed significantly on a number of issues. First, the party focused on younger cohorts and precariously employed workers in the services sector, social categories that were politically underrepresented (Tsakatika and Eleftheriou 2013: 10). Second, the 2003 programmatic congress of Synaspismos announced an end to any possibility for cooperation with PASOK and declared that the Simitis government represented "a type of consensual neo-liberalism" (Synaspismos 2003). Third, the party believed that new forms of protest and resistance were emerging; SYRIZA identified these in a variety of social movements: the Zapatistas, the counter-Summits, the World Social Forums, the peace movement, and others. All these incorporated disadvantaged classes and minorities of all kinds and origins. In the face of globalized capital, SYRIZA saw the need for—even the inevitability of—a new globalized and multifaceted Left that would offer hope for a different world, one in which people would come before profits.

In 2009, just before the outbreak of the economic crisis and amid a SYRIZA internal crisis, the Synaspismos party decided to put together a new programme (Synaspismos 2009). Later published as an impressive, almost 400-page book, it dealt with almost all aspects of public life as well as state policies (Spourdalakis 2013: 104). In the 40-page introduction outlining the ideological points, a vision of the "society of needs" was juxtaposed against the existing "society of profits," and a call to reclaim "public space" was put forward against encroaching privatization. The party's economic policy was anti-neo-liberal, vehemently opposing privatizations and usually voting down austerity-heavy state budgets. In the 2009 programme the party made proposals in the area of financial and social policy that included demands for reduced taxes, especially indirect taxes, while the well-to-do would be required to bear a greater burden; that all privatizations be repealed; and that military expenditures be immediately cut by half.

Mobilizing for a Social Europe

Despite opposition from its leftist members, Synaspismos was initially fully committed to the EU project, which the party leadership at the time saw as a promising alternative to the collapsed socialist bloc (Mpalafas 2012: 49). Gradually, Synaspismos (and later SYRIZA) called for a more "social Europe" to be maintained though its pro-Europeanism. In this way, it abstained from voting on the 1999 Amsterdam Treaty and put forth proposals for revising the Maastricht criteria, for a "social chart," and for a pan-European programme to combat unemployment. The party opposed the Constitutional Treaty, although some members of the reformist faction and one of its Members of the European Parliament (EMPs) (Papayiannakis) voted favourably in the European Parliament (EP). This stance towards European integration had been labelled as Left Europeanism (Mpelantis 2014: 227–231); that is, it was critical but not dismissive. Left Europeanism also was shown when it voted in favour of Greece's accession to the Eurozone in 2000.

Synaspismos was one of the driving forces in the party of the European Left (EL). It lead the way in the reconstitution of the European United Left in the EP in 1994 and hosted various international meetings between RLPs, with the goal of uniting all radical Left forces under a common party. They participated in the EL's founding congress in Rome in 2004 and also hosted the first EL Congress in October 2005. SYRIZA agreed with the basic consensus of the EL (see Mpalafas 2012: 287–288), and the majority of its members supported transnational involvement at the European level. This was not true of its allies; SYRIZA had a number of Eurosceptic parties, including the official Maoist Communist Organization of Greece (KOE) and the Left Platform.

SYRIZA participated actively in EU structures and networks, and the party has had close contacts with social movements such as the Association for the Taxation of Financial Transactions and Citizen's Action (ATTAC), both in Greece and in Europe—for example, in 2006

Synaspismos and ATTAC jointly organized the World Social Forum in Athens (Janssen 2013: 20). Numerous representatives of the party were also present at ensuing Social Forums (e.g., Transform 2013). SYRIZA supported the European Antifascist Manifesto (Antifascism Europe 2013) and was closely linked with a number of European RLPs, particularly the German Left Party (Die Linke), the French Left Front (FG), and the Portuguese Bloco.

POSITION IN THE PARTY SYSTEM

The electoral system in Greece has been described as "reinforced proportionality," a system that favours the strongest party. Therefore, although since 1980 the Left parties (including the social democrats) have always garnered more than 50 % of the vote, there was never the possibility of cooperation between the social democrats (PASOK) and the communists. The KKE-Es consistently enjoyed a low but stable level of support, hovering between 1.5 % and 3 % (see Table 3.1); following in this tradition, post-1991 Synaspismos maintained its presence within the Greek party spectrum at between 2 % and 2.5 % of the electorate (see Table 3.2).

Within the Left bloc, Synaspismos, and later SYRIZA, fell ideologically between the KKE and the PASOK. As PASOK moved ever closer to the European mainstream, especially since the 1990s, the KKE remained faithful to its dogma, even with the collapse of the Soviet Union. The Eurocommunist Greek Left never achieved the party goal of forming a broad alliance with the Left, as it continued to place third in the leftist political camp. The party strategy always revolved around the issue of alliances between the parties of the wider Left. Of the two greatest possible allies, PASOK and KKE, the latter rejected any such suggestion, and Synaspismos argued over cooperation with PASOK. Even so, most of the realized alliances failed to meet the expectations of those who had built them (Marioulas 2010).

After SYRIZA's creation, and particularly after the 2009 elections, the party majority held fast to the project of creating a "third pole" in society in order to achieve fundamental change; this strategy included the call to unify the entire Left. The KKE, however, saw all other parties including SYRIZA as promoting capitalism and compliance with the EU, and this was their rationale for refusing cooperation, even in the trade union movement (March 2011: 52–56). Therefore, SYRIZA charted an autonomous course mostly oriented towards the social movements and nonaligned citizens who wanted change. As SYRIZA gained in popularity during the late 2000s, the party realized that traditional bipartisanship was coming to an end; moreover, seeing its positive reception by the popular masses, SYRIZA's leadership openly appealed to disappointed PASOK voters (Eleftheriou 2015).

FROM PROTEST TO GOVERNMENT

SYRIZA was now a peculiar, rather fluid catch-all party committed to radical reform. Yet, it was unwilling to advocate the historical concept of communism or socialism to define its own social vision (Spourdalakis 2013). This can be explained by the many different audiences it appealed to and also because such a definition would undermine its capacity to influence society with more practical, day-to-day proposals. The party tried to balance between reform and revolution by building a tolerant party culture, connecting competing intraparty Left traditions. Accordingly, both Synaspismos and SYRIZA based their organizational structure on the pluralism of their various factions, combining both the old and new Left.

Pluralism, however, proved to be a double-edged sword; the many factions caused the party political division, dispute, and strife that threw the party into constant inwardness and limited its appeal. This strife was not merely pluralism of opinion; often it was a polemic resembling the Hobbesian "war of all against all." Essentially, there were many parties in one and each one refused to comprise, resulting in disappointment, inertia, and detachment, and ultimately a very negative image for the party. Synaspismos and SYRIZA never evolved into a political unit with better political cohesion, nor was it able to consolidate various organizations locally. Thus, the party experienced a number of splits during its 23-year history—most often of a "rightist" nuance. The new environment brought about by the economic crisis and the implosion of PASOK that led to SYRIZA's sudden electoral rise, created conditions for "leftist" dissent (see Chap. 6).

Throughout this period (i.e., until the early 2010s) SYRIZA was unable to capitalize on PASOK's decline or the KKE's inability to massify. The powerful bipartisanship of the Greek party system remained in place despite its obvious shortcomings and popular grievances. What triggered the massive change was the unprecedented economic crisis and its repercussions, which seemed to have given the final blow to the "old" regime of the *Metapolitefsi*. This benefitted SYRIZA electorally, of course, but it also forced the party to consider other options regarding its position and role in the political system (i.e., the pursuit of government participation).

NOTE

1. For a brief synopsis of their historical paths, see Spourdalakis (2013: 100–105).

BIBLIOGRAPHY

Alexatos, G. (2008). *Historic Dictionary of the Greek Labour Movement*, Athens: Geitonies tou Kosmou [in Greek].

Clogg, R. (1987). *Parties and Elections in Greece. The Search for Legitimacy*, Durham: Duke University Press.

Close, D. H. (1993) (Ed.). *The Greek Civil War 1943–1950*, London: Routledge.

Doukas, G. (1991) 'The thirteenth congress of the KKE: defeat of the renovators', *Journal of Communist Studies*, 7(3), pp. 393–398.

Dragasakis, Y. (2012). 'Preface', in Y. Mpalafas, *It Took 20 Years: The Chronicle of Synaspismos*, Athens: Nissos [in Greek], pp. 11–15.

Eleftheriou, C. (2015). 'The Greek Radical Left and the Crisis (2010-2015): Aspects of a Great Overturn', *Sygxrona Themata*, 130–131, December, pp. 61–73 [in Greek].

Eleftheriou, C. and Tassis, Ch. (2013). *PASOK: The Rise and Fall of a Hegemonic Party*, Athens: Savallas [in Greek].

Featherstone, K. (2005) (Eds). *Politics and Policy in Greece. The Challenge of Modernization*, London: Routledge.

Hayward, J. (1980). 'Trade Union Movements and their Politico-Economic Environments: A Preliminary Framework', pp. 1–9, in J. Hayward (Eds), *Trade Unions and Politics in Western Europe*, London: Cass.

Janssen, T. (2013). *The Parties of the Left in Europe*. Berlin: Rosa Luxembourg Stiftung.

Kalyvas, S. & Marantzidis, N. (2002) 'Greek Communism, 1968–2001', *East European Politics and Societies*, 16(3), pp. 665–690.

Kapetanyannis, B. (1979). 'The Making of Greek Eurocommunism', *Political Quarterly*, 50(4), pp. 445–460.

Kapetanyannis, B. (1993). 'The Left in the 1980s: too little, too late', in Greece 1981–1989. In R. Clogg (Ed), *The Populist Decade*, London: Macmillan Press, pp. 78–93.

Kassimeris, G. (2015). Extreme Phenomena: Violence and Terrorism in the Metapolitefsi, Athens: Kastaniotis [in Greek].

Kassimeris, G. (2001). 'Junta by Another Name? The 1974 Metapolitefsi and the Greek Extra-parliamentary Left', *Journal of Contemporary History*, 40(4), pp. 745–762.

Kotsaka, T. and Kotsonopoulos, L. (2012). 'From Crisis to Crisis: State policies and the formation of hegemonic socio-political blocs in the context of inverted democratization', Paper produced for the first phase of the Project: *Austerity policies and political representation crisis: New challenges for the Southern European Left*, Nicos Poulantzas Institute, Athens.

Lyrintzis, C. (1987). 'The Power of Populism: the Greek Case', *European Journal of Political Research*, 15(6), pp. 667–686.

Lyrintzis, C. (2005). 'The Changing Party System: Stable Democracy, Contested "Modernization"', *West European Politics*, 28(2), pp. 249–252.

Lyrintzis, C. (2011). 'Greek Politics in the Era of Economic Crisis: Reassessing Causes and Effects', Hellenic Observatory Papers on Greece and Southeast Europe, 45.

March, L. (2011). *Radical Left Parties in Europe*, London: Routledge.

Marioulas, J. (2010). 'The Greek Left', in B. Daiber, Hildebrandt, C. and Striethorst, A. (Eds), *From Revolution to Coalition: Radical Left Parties in Europe*, Berlin: Rosa Luxemburg Stiftung, pp. 292–308.

Meynaud, J. (2002). *The Political Forces in Greece 1946-1965*, Vol. I and II, Athens: Savvalas [in Greek].

Mpalafas, Y. (2012). *It Took 20 Years: The Chronicle of Synaspismos*, Athens: Nissos [in Greek].

Mpelantis, D. (2014). *The Left and Power: The "Democratic Way" to Socialism*, Athens: Topos [in Greek].

Mpenas, T. (2011), *The Greek 1968. Contribution to the History of the KKE Interior*, Athens: Themelio [in Greek].

Papademetriou, G. and Spourdalakis, M. (1994). *The Statutes of Political Parties*, Athens-Komotini: Sakkoulas [in Greek].

Pridham, G. and Verney, S. (1991). 'The coalitions of 1989 –90 in Greece: inter-party relations and Democratic Consolidation', *West European Politics*, 14(4), pp. 42–69.

Spourdalakis, M. (2013), 'Left Strategy in the Greek Cauldron: Explaining SYRIZA's Success', in L. Panitch, G. Albo and V. Chibber (Eds), *Socialist Register 2013: The Question of Strategy*, London: Merlin Press, pp. 98–120.

Spourdalakis, M. (2003). 'The Political Parties Phenomenon: Evolution and Context', in D. Tsatsos and X. Doxiades (Eds) The Future of Political Parties, Athens: Papazisis, pp. 39–64 [in Greek].

Spourdalakis, M. (Eds) (1998). *PASOK. Party – State - Society*. Athens: Patakis [in Greek].

Spourdalakis, M. (1988), *The Rise of the Greek Socialist Party*, London: Routledge.

Stavrakakis, Y. and Katsambekis, G. (2014). 'Left-wing Populism in the European Periphery: the case of Syriza', *Journal of Political Ideologies*, 19(2), pp. 119–142.

Synaspismos (2009), *For the 21st Century Left*, Athens.

Synaspismos (2005). N. Chountis speech at the Organizational Conference, http://www.syn.gr/gr/keimeno.php?id=7156, Accessed 21 September 2015.

Synaspismos (2004), Political Resolution of the 4th Congress, http://www.syn.gr/downloads/apofasi4ou.pdf, accessed 22 September 2015.

Synaspismos (2003). Programmatic Directions, http://www.syn.gr/downloads/program2003.pdf, accessed 22 September 2015.

Synaspismos (2000), Political Resolution of the 3rd Congress, http://www.syn.gr/downloads/apofasi3ou.pdf, accessed 22 September 2015.

Synaspismos (1992). The Political resolution of Synaspismos 1st Congress], available online at: http://www.syn.gr/gr/keimeno.php?idO13386

SYRIZA (2013). The Statute of SYRIZA, July.

Teperoglou, E. and Tsatsanis, E. (2014), 'Dealignment, Delegitimation and the Implosion of the Two-Party System in Greece: The Earthquake Election of 6 May 2012', *Journal of Elections, Public Opinion and Parties*, 24(2), pp. 222–242.

Transform! Europe (2013). transform! Europe at the WSF 2013 – Programme: transform-network.net/calendar/calendar-2013/news/detail/Calendar/-6901265lea.html.

Tsakatika, M. and Eleftheriou, C. (2013), 'The Radical Left's Turn towards Civil Society in Greece: One Strategy, Two Paths', *South European Society and Politics*, 18(1), pp. 81–99.

Vernardakis, C. (2011). *Political Parties, Elections and the Party System: The Transformations of Political Representation 1990-2010*, Athens: Sakkoulas [in Greek].

Vernardakis, C. (2006). '1990-1993. Internal Politics', Chapter 9, in *History of the Greeks. Contemporary Hellenism: From 1949 To Date*, Vol. 14, Athens: Domi, pp. 325–346.

Vernardakis, C. and Mavris, Y. (1991). Parties and Social Alliances in Pre-Dictatorial Greece, Athens: Exantas [in Greek].

Verney, S. (2014). 'Broken and Can't be Fixed': The Impact of the Economic Crisis on the Greek Party System', *The International Spectator*, 49(1), pp. 18–35.

Verney, S. (1989). '"Compromesso storico": Reunion and Renewal on the Greek Left', *Journal of Communist Studies*, 5(4), pp. 200–206.

CHAPTER 4

AKEL's Twofold Legacy

Abstract This chapter contains first a brief overview of AKEL's origins and development that highlight a blend of Marxism-Leninism ideology with social democratic/labourite political practice. It then examines in depth the way in which the party changed both ideologically and organizationally subsequent to the dissolution of the socialist bloc. The changes that AKEL introduced opened the way for the party to strive for executive office, as it responded to the two dimensions necessary for achieving democratic legitimacy: the subjective (the party's own initiatives for change) and the objective (whether the other parties perceived the change).

Keywords Communist Party of Cyprus • AKEL • Organization • Ideology • Popular movement • Elections

Unlike other communist parties in South Europe, the Progressive Party of Working People (AKEL) could never really be described as an anti-systemic party. The size of the party; its long practice of coalition-building, especially at the local level; and its support for the centrist presidents of Cyprus differentiated AKEL in this respect and served to make it an influential political actor. It was considered to be anti-regime by the other Cypriot political forces, however, and was never really accepted as an equal government partner, similar to all communist parties of South Europe. The party consistently was excluded from cabinet participation, being viewed primarily as a vote carrier; changing this perception in the aftermath of the 1990

© The Editor(s) (if applicable) and The Author(s) 2016
Y. Katsourides, *Radical Left Parties in Government*,
DOI 10.1057/978-1-137-58841-8_4

events was considered crucial for its survival and success and, consequently, its chance for exercise of power.

To fully understand the exceptional case of AKEL in Cyprus, however, we must look at the history of both the party and the island (e.g., the long-standing unresolved Cyprus Problem[1]). Both factors worked in favour of the party's efforts towards repositioning.

THE CYPRIOT LEFT IN HISTORY (1926–1990)

The party's roots date to the 1920s. Founded in 1926 as the Communist Party of Cyprus (CPC) by a group of radical intellectuals and workers influenced by Russia's October Revolution, it then was the oldest party on the island that represented the working class and the underprivileged strata of the population (Katsourides 2014a). It opposed British rule and, despite its small size, actively participated in the anti-colonial uprising that shook the island in 1931. Whereas the Church and the island's emerging Greek bourgeoisie advocated *enosis* (i.e., the union of Cyprus with Greece), the CPC called for political independence and socialism. This was not unrelated to the ethnic composition of Cyprus (82 % Greeks and 18 % Turks), as well as the party's opposition to the ruling class's demand for enosis, which the party saw as a ploy for the further consolidation of bourgeois domination.

The party's perception of the Russian Revolution as a historical step forward, together with its view of the Soviet Union as an ally of the struggling Cypriot working class, created a strong ideological umbrella under which the first partisans challenged the entire structure of the Greek Cypriot ruling classes (Panayiotou 2006: 275). Organizing underground in the 1930s, the CPC channeled its activities into founding the island's trade union movement—a significant difference from other European parties of the working class (e.g., the British Labour Party). In Cyprus, it was the communists that initiated the trade union movement, thereby establishing their historical affiliation and tutelage over it. During this period, Cypriot communists who fled the island for Britain and the United States constituted proportionally the largest contingent of international volunteers in the Spanish Civil War (Strongos 2010). Throughout this period, though, the CPC was never able to gain mass support within Cypriot society and remained on the margins (Katsourides 2014a: 164–172).

This situation changed in the early 1940s, when in 1941 the CPC was rebranded as the AKEL in order to escape colonial proscription. Founded initially as a "popular front" organization, the party included "progressive bourgeois elements"; and in November 1944 it also incorporated the clandestine CPC, not without a reaction (Katsourides 2014a: 190–191). AKEL was actually a diverse movement molded along the model of the Popular Fronts of the 1930s (Panayiotou 2014: 10).

In the immediate post-war period AKEL figured prominently in several class confrontations, which united workers from both the Greek and the Turkish Cypriot communities and culminated in a series of major strikes in 1948 (PEO 1979). These actions led to the silent withdrawal of the party's more liberal elements because, in the domestic context, party ideology was considered highly subversive and revolutionary. In fact, compared to the CPC, the party's philosophy was actually reformist in both its rhetoric and its programmes (Charalambous 2012a: 155).

AKEL very purposefully was established to be a mass party organization—one that would be highly integrated into society. The party achieved success by following a strategy that was compromising to the political forces as well as appealing to a large segment of the society. Thus, rather than "revolution," the party decided to pursue the electoral "road to power"; to this end, they sought alliances with centre and centre-right political parties and personalities. The second part of this strategy focused on a broad conceptualization of the Left so that party policies and stances spoke not only to blue-collar workers/labourers but also to the middle class (Katsourides 2012: 191). As a result, since the 1940s the party has been part of local-level coalitions (Protopapas 2012) and has earned the firm support of close to one-third of the Cypriot population; this indicates that it is not a party of a constituency or a subculture. AKEL's supporters can be found in all social classes, even if its support is greatest among the wage-dependent sector.

AKEL's organizational structure, which was established and institutionalized during the 1940s, can be best described as a series of concentric circles with the party at its heart; it incorporates broad segments of society—that is, the largest trade union of Cyprus (Pancyprian Federation of Labour, PEO); organizations for youth (United Democratic Youth Organization, EDON), farmers (Union of Cypriot Farmers, EKA), and women (Pancyprian Federation of Women's Organization, POGO); and cultural and athletic associations, which are present in every community and village in the country. All these groups provide AKEL with a robust mechanism for mobilization, and together they comprise the so-called Popular Movement (*Laiko Kinima*). All AKEL auxiliary organizations have considerable operational autonomy, but they take ideological and political guidance from the party (Ellinas and Katsourides 2013). Within the party, democratic centralism has been the overarching organizational principle.

Unlike its predecessor the CPC, AKEL endorsed enosis because it believed that party could work as part of a new strategy against colonialism (Katsourides 2014b: 482–483; Leventis 2002); thus, AKEL not only joined but also led the anti-colonial battle, seeing it as a mass political struggle. The party recognized that the island's liberation from British rule required cooperation with other political groupings and necessitated shifting alliances. For this reason, AKEL felt class collaboration was justified, and it also felt that a bourgeois democracy would be necessary before the transition to socialism.

The defeat of the communists in the Greek Civil War (1946–1949) signalled the beginning of an era in which the Right took the reins in internal political life in Cyprus under Archbishop Makarios, especially through the 1955–1959 armed struggle of EOKA (i.e., the National Organization of Cypriot Fighters) (Alimi et al. 2012). This culminated in the establishment of the Republic of Cyprus with Makarios its first president. For its role in the anti-colonial battle, and despite opposing the EOKA, AKEL was outlawed by the colonial administration in 1955 (Katsourides 2014b: 491); it was legalized only when the independent state of Cyprus was founded in 1960.

The party's historical path led to the emergence of a number of characteristics, the effects of which still are being felt (Marioulas 2010: 366). For example, we can see how the subculture of the party was shaped by the labour and liberation struggles. From the outset, the leadership worked to inculcate a sense of class-consciousness among the working people. The fact that the party leadership had been persecuted, and that the party itself had been banned during British colonialism, led AKEL to establish and maintain a strict democratic centralist policy—to the extent of creating a personality cult—to ensure discipline among its members. The party defined its anti-imperialism according to Soviet terminology and kept its international relations within the confines of the Soviet sphere, all the while avoiding any dealings with reformist communist parties (Adams 1971: 156–179).

AKEL's political identity has been characterized by anti-capitalist, anti-European Economic Community (EEC), and anti-NATO postures; anti-nationalist sentiments; and close relations with the Turkish Cypriot community. This legacy has continued into the mid-2010s. The experience of exclusion, discrimination, and derision by the establishment, together with AKEL's practice of class collaboration, has shaped the political makeup of the party's huge base.

POSITION IN THE PARTY SYSTEM

AKEL opposed the founding agreements of the Republic of Cyprus primarily because of their concessions to Turkey, Britain, and NATO, and in the first presidential election of 1959 presented its own candidate to stand against Makarios who had signed the agreements. When Makarios, however, looked to the Soviet Union and the Arab world for arms and diplomatic support (given the West's unresponsiveness towards Greek Cypriot demands), the AKEL became more supportive of the Archbishop. In fact, throughout the 1960s the two agreed more and more on policy issues, as Makarios gradually lost enthusiasm for enosis and acted to strengthen the independent Republic of Cyprus. During this period, the country became a member of the Non-Aligned Movement, and Makarios enlarged parts of the welfare state and expanded the size of the public sector.

With independence Cyprus's political system was completely restructured, and the constitutional weight assigned to the president's office was the new government's most salient feature (Ker-Lindsay 2008). Moreover, the constitution stipulated that the president was to be elected directly by the people. The AKEL party realized the power vested in the presidential office and adopted a strategy that recognized this, offering support to Makarios in exchange for a nonaligned international policy. It also understood that political parties had to seek alliances with each other because no single party could gain the presidency on its own. Since 1974 the most crucial determinant of these alliances has been the Cyprus Problem; in fact, this "problem" has dictated the entire political life of the island. It also explains why AKEL decided not to pursue a socialist agenda (AKEL 1962, 1978: 18); the Cyprus Problem offered the party a way to justify marginalizing its socialist programme, as they could ideologically locate it within a stagist approach.

The Republic of Cyprus was established on an unworkable constitution, one that effectively divided the country rather than uniting it. Thus, barely three years after independence, intercommunal tension—for the most part instigated by foreign powers—was high and often resulted in violence. In 1974 a Greek junta-led coup was the signal for a Turkish invasion and occupation of the northern part of Cyprus. Since then the country has been divided along ethnic lines, and its politics have been consumed by this state of affairs. Because many extreme rightists and people who supported the coup found shelter in the right-wing Democratic Rally party (DISY), which was established in 1976, DISY was isolated and discredited.

This was the opening AKEL had been waiting for; now the party could enforce a new strategy that it named "alliance of the democratic forces." By means of this strategy, the party secured programmatic agreements as well as ministerial portfolios for nonmembers. Under it AKEL approached the centre-right Democratic Party (DIKO) and the socialist United Democratic Union of the Centre (EDEK), while it identified DISY as the main ideological opponent. In fact, ever since Cyprus's independence, the party had been pursuing a democratic integration strategy—one that took the form of influencing the government rather than exercising power.

Since its establishment AKEL has been in a dominant position among the Cypriot Left. Although the right-wing political forces were fragmented until 1976 (Katsourides 2013), the Left, which had been dominated by AKEL since the 1920s, was solid. There was no threat to AKEL from the Left because prior to 1969 there was no Cypriot socialist party, and the social democratic party, EDEK, was fairly ineffectual. Moreover, there was no far Left party. The only serious threat to the party came on the eve of the dissolution of the socialist bloc in 1989 when a group of AKEL dissidents formed the Renewed Democratic Socialist Movement (ADISOK); however, this party proved short-lived and merged with another party in 1996.

AKEL has been the only communist party that has continuously dominated the political Left in the European Union (EU) member state since 1990, and up to the early 2010s it consistently has polled more than 30 % (Table 4.1). Although the density of the party's support (i.e., the ratio of members to voters) has decreased over the last 20 years, it nevertheless remains very high especially compared to other South Europe parties (Charalambous 2012b). However, any effort to understand AKEL's mass appeal also must consider the Cyprus Problem. Support for AKEL did not depend exclusively on whether voters supported socialism or liberalism; instead, it was mediated by all parties' positions regarding that problem (Ellinas and Katsourides 2013). AKEL drew support from those who, while not necessarily committed to the Left, supported the communist position in the Cyprus conflict.

Table 4.1   AKEL's electoral performance in parliamentary elections, 1981–2011

Election year	Votes	%	Seats
1981	95,364	32.77	12
1985	87,628	27.43	15
1991	104,771	30.63	18
1996	121,958	33.00	19
2001	142,648	34.71	20
2006	131,066	31.13	18
2011	132,163	32.67	19

Source: Ministry of Interior

Note: Elections prior to 1981 were held under a majoritarian electoral system that encouraged coalition-building, thereby making comparisons invalid

For the two decades that followed the 1974 catastrophe, the "political contract" between AKEL and the "progressive centre-right" predominated. AKEL became the electoral pillar of every single government elected from then until 1993, yet it had no direct participation in any government even though it enjoyed a huge mass base and electorate. This was put in jeopardy in the mid- and late-1980s after a combination of internal and external events threatened party unity, obligating the party to take action.

THE FALL OF THE USSR AND AKEL'S RESPONSE

The dissolution of the socialist camp was not the sole motive for change. AKEL's electoral defeat in 1985, which the party attributed to its tacit cooperation with the right-wing DISY (AKEL 1986), caused a huge internal crisis in terms of both party ideology and the most appropriate party model. The "reformists" asked for large-scale reforms and called for "de-Stalinization" and an end to "monolithic" attitudes and leadership (Charalambous 2007: 431). The crisis was intensified by the fact that it coincided with a change in party leadership (Katsourides 2012: 193). The upheaval ended with the orthodox communist line (and candidate) prevailing and the internal opposition leaving the party. Those who departed included some of the most influential figures of the Left at the time; they went on to form the new party (i.e., ADISOK). Although this offshoot was short-lived, the matter proved that even within parties of democratic centralism, such as AKEL, conflict and factionalism can occur.

Because of this internal crisis, however, AKEL was in a position to respond to the external situation (i.e., dissolution of the soviet bloc); in other words, the party was in a state of readiness and well able to withstand the external shock and react opportunely. The party instigated changes to its rules, policies, strategies, and tactics that aimed: (1) to reposition AKEL in the Cypriot political and party systems in such a way that the party would be viewed as an acceptable political actor, and (2) to preserve the party's radical identity and socialist vision. At the same time, though, the changes raised the eternal question regarding the communist character of the party.

In 1990 AKEL convened a congress at which a new ideological manifesto was presented; it promoted a much more pragmatic and eclectic stance. The manifesto called for a rejection of those Soviet policies that limited democracy (i.e., Stalinism) and prevented economic development, while acknowledging the social and workers' achievements in the USSR for their contribution to the working-class movement worldwide. The manifesto, which was titled "Our Perception of Socialism," emphasized the contributions the party had made to the island throughout its history, calling on Cypriots to judge AKEL without reference to the Soviet model.

The pragmatism evidenced in this manifesto was directly linked to the Cyprus Problem. AKEL realized that in order to have a chance at power it had to propose something agreeable to other parties' solution to the problem, which meant it had to concede some of its ideology. For this reason, although AKEL had always worked for a solution to the Cyprus Problem in an anti-NATO context, it also recognized the need to go along with the dominant Western position in the southeastern Mediterranean. In the post-1990 era the party also understood that it was important to deemphasize its socialist agenda, as in this way it could more easily survive politically. AKEL therefore downplayed the class divide and its socialist policies and emphasized that it was a "national" political party for all Cypriots. This new stance allowed AKEL to remain a powerful political actor.

Organization

The party undertook organizational changes aimed in two directions: (1) to enhance internal democracy and promote members' involvement in political decision making at all levels, and (2) to obtain a more flexible party structure that would be able to adapt to the changing environment.

To this end, a series of changes were initiated (AKEL 1991a: 10–11)—for example, arenas for member participation were introduced (e.g., secret voting was established for intraparty elections), and candidates for public offices had to be recommended by party cells and nominated by district assemblies. A few years later a ceiling of three terms for some public offices (e.g., MPs) was mandated (AKEL 2005). Public debate prior to congresses, both by members in party cells and through the party press, was inaugurated and remains in place to this day.

Such changes made only a negligible impact on the party's Leninist organizational character, with the party's congress still the highest authority and democratic centralism the founding principle. With the basic principles unchanged, the party continued to be safeguarded against a number of both external (e.g., careful selection of members) and internal threats to its organization (e.g., prohibiting candidate rankings for the Central Committee). The statute (AKEL 2011a) continued to explicitly prohibit the formation of any type of faction within AKEL and adhered to its strict policy of expelling members who refused to comply with the binding decisions of the majority. Membership in the Central Committee was still heavily weighted in favour of party officials and employees, as well as cadres of the auxiliary organizations, with the party's organizational machine remaining something of a "machine for domination" (Althusser 1978: 26).

Nevertheless, the initial positive effects of these changes were later negated by structural ineffectiveness evident in some aspects of the party's organization (Ellinas and Katsourides 2013). These included the following: low levels of members' participation, rarer contributions in public debates, dual mandates in internal bodies, and slow internal decision making. One of the most negative tendencies was the decline in active membership; in the five years preceding the party's 21st Congress, on average only 41 % of members attended party-cell meetings (AKEL 2010a: 3). Moreover, the more relaxed internal organization led to reduced control and less self-discipline (AKEL 1994: 12). This proved harmful to the party's character over time because it implied a different motive for engaging in party affairs; increasingly, members used the party to secure both elected and appointed state offices (Ellinas and Katsourides 2013).

In spite of these difficulties, AKEL managed to preserve its basic organizational structure, adjusting it in ways that reinforced its organizational capacity. In contrast to the organizational decay evident in some of its western European counterparts, AKEL managed to sustain its dense network of party base units and party cells, which totaled 535 in 2007—approximately, one cell per 1500 inhabitants of Cyprus. Moreover, these party base units were almost totally active, as 93 % of them held annual general assemblies (AKEL 2007).

The organizational stability of the party also was confirmed by membership figures, which indicated that membership remained stable at around 14,000 (AKEL 1991a, 2010a). Party data shows that the vast majority of the members, about 89 %, diligently paid their dues. As a percentage of the overall votes AKEL had been receiving in parliamentary elections, the membership density of the party experienced a notable decline; however, this can be explained to some extent by the party's strict recruitment policy—that is, it ensured that the party remained united and that new members were committed to the party's ideology. To promote this, AKEL undertook the education of new party members through lectures, seminars, and courses (AKEL 1994, 2015a).

Also key to AKEL's stability was the power invested in official party bodies. In fact, the extraparliamentary component of AKEL has been considerably more powerful than the party's parliamentary caucus, which accepts all Congress and Central Committee decisions, with only a few minor exceptions. This attitude was contrary to international trends, where the state was becoming more influential in the dissemination of party resources (Katz and Mair 1995). The dominance of the extraparliamentary also was evident from the composition of the politburo of AKEL, which was largely made up of permanent party officials who did not hold public office or a parliamentary seat.

In the late 1980s, AKEL's relationship with the popular movement was tested, most clearly evidenced in the party affiliation with the trade union (i.e., PEO). Ultimately, however, AKEL decided to maintain its ties to the trade union, thus preserving a key component of its organizational model. The four organizations employed hundreds of paid officials—all party members—who on a daily basis acted as intermediaries between the party and its voters. Its commitment to the popular movement offered AKEL significant organizational advantages (Ellinas and Katsourides 2013) by reinforcing the party's political authority in society, communicating party messages to the wide membership base of the auxiliary organizations, furnishing the party with an efficient mechanism for recording voter preferences, and offering a large pool from which to recruit new party members.

Overall, therefore, AKEL kept its Leninist character by maintaining the "centralist" elements of its organizational structure, thus highlighting the importance of stability and continuity of a party organization.

Ideology and Programme

Arguably, the greatest difficulty for communist parties is to maximize votes while remaining loyal to Marxism-Leninism. The ideological changes AKEL endorsed had two primary purposes. First, they aimed to reposition themselves within the Cyprus party system; that is, they would demonstrate their democratic credentials, proving their potential as a viable coalition partner. This required several important modifications including the acceptance of multipartyism and democratic succession in power, a commitment to the democratic way to socialism, and the decision to accept social democrats as strategic allies. A second aim was to outline their own (vague) version of socialism; this included the separation of powers in the functioning of the state, the doctrine of a mixed economy, recognition of a need for diversity in socialist development along with multiple modes of ownership, opposition to the dictatorship of any class, and an emphasis on human and democratic rights (AKEL 1990, 1991a).

In effect, these changes pointed to the party's official, although unspoken, acceptance of Eurocommunism or even classic social democracy. However, their ideology differed from the latter on two important issues: (1) the party clearly distanced itself from governing social democratic parties and drew a clear line between the two ideological stances (AKEL 1990: 2); and (2) the AKEL reaffirmed its commitment to an (eventual) transition to socialism, as opposed to classical social democracy. The party still remained a Marxist-Leninist one (AKEL 2015c) and, as such, envisioned the transformation of society. Under pressure for more openness and fearing that the changes could impinge on the party's ideological and political unity and identity, AKEL made a greater effort to ensure the ideological education of its members and, to this end, established both a school and a research institute (AKEL 2010b: 48).

The party always had believed that policy and strategy should be country-specific and so by dismissing Stalinism and combining Marxism-Leninism and social democratic theory, it managed to shake off the image of a hardline communist party and appeal to those beyond its core supporters. The party very successfully coupled its vision for change with the need for reform within the Cypriot social system. Although still modelled on Leninist organizational principles, AKEL actually operated according to a form of statism much closer to the social democratic tradition. Thus, with time, the party's Marxist-Leninist philosophy weakened aside from when addressing core supporters.

There were no objections to these changes, one obvious reason being the members' realization of their disadvantageous position—a position in which all communist parties found themselves during that period. Another reason was the consensual character of Cypriot politics, which had essentially nullified any type of social protest (Charalambous 2014) as a result of Europeanization (Katsourides 2003) and the "Code of Industrial Relations." The latter, essentially a "social contract" between labour and capital, was based on the unofficial institution of tripartite cooperation and collective negotiations between the state, the trade unions, and employers' associations (Sparsis 1998).

Yet, there were also important internal factors at play. First, AKEL never really discussed theoretical issues, thus avoiding heated debates and the problems usually associated with them. Theoretical work always lagged behind its practice (Charalambous 2007). Therefore, with a lack of discussion or debate, it was not surprising that AKEL never "produced" any significant theoretical texts, analyses, or prominent intellectuals. This lack of ideological debate also reflected a rather superficial or better instinctive adherence to Marxism-Leninism. Second, throughout the party's history the authority of party leadership, whether cultivated, enforced, or even actually proven, had never been open to discussion. Therefore, effecting important changes was always a matter of a top-down approach; that is, whoever controlled the leadership could dictate the "correct" form of Marxism.

Despite the ideological changes, there remained important aspects of continuity, especially the party's attachment to symbolic events and the rhetoric of the past. AKEL acknowledged that a sudden break with its own past would result in an ideological and organizational collapse, so the founding date of the CPC in 1926, May Day, and the anniversary of the Russian Revolution are celebrated every year as important symbols; and they also provide the members with a sense of continuity. The party positioned itself as a modernizing force, albeit one with a proud tradition on which the party's leadership successfully drew as a resource rather than as a constraint (Dunphy and Bale 2007: 139, 142).

Even though Marxist-Leninist ideology has remained crucial for the leadership and the party's core members, the party's public rhetoric includes many elements of liberalism (Peristianis 2006: 258–259).

AKEL has placed less emphasis on its Marxist roots since the changes were effected, focusing more on the regulation of a social market. It used an increasingly softened communist rhetoric together with a tendency to tone issues down or up—generally in accordance with the electoral circumstances. This was largely due to the salience of electioneering for the entire party structure. Ideological changes were reflected in programmatic positions as well, which were infused with "pragmatism"; the party watered-down any references to nationalizations and radical modifications to the tax system, and it elevated issues of the welfare state. Throughout the 1990s, AKEL aimed to revive the basic tenets of the "social contract." It defended the institutionalized "tripartite dialogue" between the three actors, which resolved every instance of severe class conflict since independence—in sharp contrast to Greece—on a supposed basis of no winners and no losers.

In 2000 AKEL adopted its own version of "modernization," proposing changes to all aspects of politics and institutions. Apparently influenced by the Greek PASOK project, as well as its evident endorsement by certain social groups in Cyprus, mostly of middle-class origins, AKEL introduced its own concept of modernization; it was an effort to capitalize on an external source of legitimation that could offer competitive advantages in the Cypriot party system. Coming from a party that had not been involved in governing until then, the modernization thesis was seen as a vehicle for further (electoral) success. The project was presented as a party document at the 19th Party Congress in 2000 (AKEL 2000).

The document was primarily intended to respond to the emerging legitimacy crisis of political institutions and instances of corruption. At the same time, it was an attack on neo-liberal globalization, which the party viewed as accelerating these phenomena. Although Cyprus-framed it maintained some basic features of the respective Greek plan; most important was its emphasis on technocratic approaches, while deemphasizing ideological approaches. For example, as proclaimed in this chapter's introductory section, the aim of AKEL's proposal was to improve not only working-class conditions but also the situation of small- and mid-sized entrepreneurs (AKEL 2000: 3). Moreover, it had a specific section addressing the Cyprus stock exchange in which it demanded the introduction of mutual funds and motivation strategies for foreign investors (AKEL 2000: 23–24).

The end product of the changes was a blurry ideology, hovering between Marxism-Leninism and social democracy but maintaining an electorally crucial continuity with its past and balancing between various ideological currents accommodated within the party (Charalambous 2007: 436). This was probably due not only to the pressing circumstances but also to AKEL's mass heterogeneous electorate, which was comprised of various social groups. In the aftermath of the 1990 changes, the party underplayed the ideology factor. It has not reexamined its ideological manifesto, has avoided internal discussions on crucial ideological issues, and has not reestablished its theoretical journal (*Neos Democratis*), which ceased publication in 2001. AKEL also has avoided clarifying its precise ideological location, resorting to vague references instead. Ideological issues were always framed "in perspective," meaning that national situational factors were not suitable for a change of the system, thus dictating a realpolitik. Although significantly radical in relational terms, party ideology was not insurrectionist (Peristianis 2006).

The most critical of all changes, though, was the party's stance vis-à-vis the EU and the process of integration that involved a major premise of the party's ideological legacy.

Changing the EU Position

AKEL always has advised against EU membership, considering it a project for advanced capitalist integration that threatened both the achievements of the Left at the national level and also future radical ambitions (AKEL 1986: 105–107, 1991a: 101). It was additionally regarded as an extension of NATO and a threat to Cyprus's economic competitiveness. The party position changed in 1995, and to understand why, we must look to the national context and party competition. Following the collapse of the socialist bloc, AKEL's EU stance softened, likely out of fear of international isolation and national de-legitimation of its policies (AKEL 1991c).

In 1995, the party finally agreed to Cyprus's EU accession course without changing its opinion of the EU as a capitalist organization (AKEL 1995b: 41–44). The decision was justified based on the absence of any realistic alternatives after the collapse of the socialist bloc, the fact that almost all remaining communist parties accepted this new reality, and the possibility that Cyprus's accession could help with movement towards a reunited Cyprus through EU pressure on Turkey. In addition, joining it might provide a common target with the Turkish Cypriots and a sense of security against Turkey. The overall positive public opinion for Cyprus's membership (AKEL constituency not excluded), and fear of isolation because all other political forces were in favour of EU accession were also crucial factors in the party's decision. AKEL seemed to have accepted the EU as a necessary evil: "[T]he question of real and practical importance is not a simple yes or no to the EU, but under what terms and conditions this will materialize" (AKEL 1996).

Clearly, the decision to endorse Cyprus's EU accession was a strategic decision made by the leadership, which realized that there was no other option. This was a policy issue in a national context, and AKEL's rejection could threaten party survival and coalition potential; ideology had to take a backseat. It also proved the lengths to which the AKEL would go to have an influence on important decisions in the national domain (Peristianis 2006: 260). Commitment to Europe was used to legitimize a certain rupture with the party's traditional ideology; these included AKEL's acceptance of the free market and the necessary reinforcement of competition as part of the EU harmonization process. Still, the fact that no party besides AKEL ever professed an anti-EU position, either on the Left or the far right of the ideological spectrum, led many EU opponents to find comfort in the more concerned approach professed by AKEL.

AKEL's switch to supporting the island's EU entry can be explained by the overriding national importance of the Cyprus Problem, which also was helpful to AKEL in its desire to reposition the party; the focus on the ethnic rather than the class divide in terms of the Cyprus Problem made it easier for the party to consent to the EU perspective. It also made it easier—even though it was still quite difficult—to convince party members to espouse the new line. Although the party elite favoured the change of position, the grassroots members were more skeptical or opposed to it—60 % in favour versus 40 % opposed at the 18th Party Congress (AKEL 1996).

When AKEL began its transformation, the prime motivation was strategic. The "transformation," however, seems to be an ongoing process and has created its own momentum, sometimes with uncertain or "undesired" outcomes that conflict with party ideology. One such instance is the impacts of Europeanization, which promoted consensus (Ladrech 2001: 5) and further limiting the discretion available to parties and governments (Mair 1997: 133). The effect of Europeanization on political life in Cyprus can be seen if we look at the harmonization process. Once AKEL agreed to endorse EU accession, support from political parties was unanimous and a significant level of consensus was reached. As a result, 614 of the 620 bills concerning harmonization presented by the end of 2002 were passed unanimously (Katsourides 2003: 17).

Although unanimity increases the stability of the political system, it simultaneously increases the perceived homogenization of parties, thus erasing the distinctiveness of them; this is the case with AKEL, which throughout the party's history claimed its difference as one of its most precious assets. Europeanization significantly influenced party policies towards de-radicalization, and this is related in part to the socialization of AKEL's cadres within the EU. AKEL involvement has given party members experience with and an understanding of the EU, but it also has contributed to its further incorporation in the EU system.

In this regard, the Europeanization process triggered organizational changes, which fostered new relationships with European institutions and other networks. AKEL strengthened its relationships with the Greek Synaspismos (SYRIZA's predecessor) and became a member of the New European Left Forum and the GUE/NGL. Yet, the impact of Europeanization has had mixed results—for example, AKEL's relationship with the Party of the European Left (EL). AKEL rejected, until today full membership in the EL and retained the status of observer for two important reasons (Katsourides 2012). First, AKEL opposed several ideological and organizational principles held by the EL (e.g., the right of movements and individuals to become members). Second, EL membership, the AKEL felt, inhibits unity among Left parties because some of the largest communist parties of Europe do not participate.

In trying to maintain a balanced position between the two opposing tendencies in the European Left movement (i.e., the more hardline communists and the radical leftists), AKEL continued to have only limited dealings with the EL. Likewise, the impact of the EL on the party's policies has been minimal. Generally, the AKEL concurred with vague slogans promoted by the EL against neo-liberalism and austerity, as well as with its vision for an alternative Europe. However, it has not actively participated in any of the EL's joint projects.

AKEL's about-face on the EU issue was guided by its assertion "to fight the system from within"; that is, it would join the EU with the intention of reforming the union into a democratic and worker-friendly institution. This position, however, revealed a naïve perception of the EU and the impact that the party (and the country) could have on the system. Furthermore, European Union membership is a two-way street, and the EU can dictate policies that deviate from AKEL's popular character. For example, while AKEL continued to advocate against privatizations, it had

to agree in 2011 to the termination of some semi-governmental organizations as part of an austerity package (*Haravgi*, 14 November 2011).

In recent years, AKEL has defined itself as a party that favours a "social"
Europe, and it has promoted the rights of labour, immigrants, and other less
well-off strata of society (AKEL 2009a). The party has called for a reorientation of the EU along more interventionist lines to include the following:
emphasis on public health and education systems, opposition to privatization of (many) public facilities, among others. The party also requested a
redefinition of the European Central Bank's (ECB) tasks in the direction
of stimulating growth, fighting against unemployment, and demanding
political oversight of its workings. The preceding were reflected in AKEL's
negative vote on a number of important EU treaties: the Constitutional
Treaty, the Stability Pact, and the Bolkenstein directive, among others.

AKEL objected loudly to certain (political) features of the Lisbon
Treaty, although the party did not oppose the principle of a "political"
Europe. It was the stipulations regarding NATO and militarism that did
not sit well with AKEL, as well as the EU's lack of internal democracy
(AKEL 2009b). Still, it must be noted, paradoxically, that Christofias
as President of the Republic and previously AKEL's party chief, agreed
to stronger EU–NATO relationship at the December 2008 European
Council meeting.

AKEL's congressional and electoral manifestos offered insight into the
logic underlying party positioning depending on the audience (Katsourides
2014c). Although AKEL primarily has been critical of the EU, the congressional documents addressed to core activists were more ideologically
loaded than the electoral manifestos, which were very mild and aimed to
convey a sense of safety to the electorate.

Overall, the party's policies and public rhetoric throughout the years
sent out mixed messages. The party seemed to criticize some EU policies
and accept others in an effort to differentiate AKEL from other Cypriot
parties. The party used a strategy of asking for delays and time extensions
to harmonize Cyprus's legislation with the European directives, with no
mention of the party's stance on these policies (Charalambous 2012b)—
for example, AKEL asked for a year's delay in entering the Eurozone
(AKEL 2006). Nevertheless, a larger question arose, to which the party
has never given a definite answer; that is, would the fight to change the
EU from within be a more Marxist or a more social democratic project
(Charalambous 2007: 433)?

Electoral Strategy

The new, highly competitive campaign environment, as this was defined by the decreased role of ideology and the advent of the private media as well as changes in the traditional working-class constituency, required a modified strategy. So, in the 1991 elections AKEL presented its new electoral platform, the *AKEL-Left New Forces* (AKEL 1991a: 15). This put into practice the politics of "enlargement," which was a recognition of the party's need to appeal to the middle classes (AKEL 1991a: 10, 1995a: 35, 2001: 53) and to recruit candidates from outside the membership pool, as well as leftists from outside the party. At the same time, the party initiated a process of massive generational turnover of all faces of party organization (AKEL 1991b), signifying one of the party's key tactical manoeuvres in its effort to soften its image and position itself as a "rejuvenation force." Turnover in important party organs has continued to be relatively high, although this decreases as individuals move up the hierarchy ladder.

As part of its strategy to extend the party's popular appeal, beginning in the year 2000, AKEL began to cooperate with minor political groups—for example, Front for the Restoration of the Center (EPALXI) and United Democrats (EDH). The groups with which AKEL cooperated were ideologically to the party's right, indicating both an effort to expand its electoral appeal but also to further de-radicalization. Moreover, AKEL introduced a new concept of campaigning whereby indoor meetings and cultural events gradually replaced the mass rallies of the past, and the leader himself was placed in a prominent position (Christophorou 2001: 107). In recognition of the new media environment the party began to employ communication specialists despite the emphasis still placed on the party's machinery and canvassing (Christophorou 2006: 527). Finally, AKEL realized that in order to promote the party's policy to a wider audience (AKEL 1994: 24, 2010b: 43, 2015b: 36, 76), it was necessary to become involved in the new emerging civil society sector and also to embrace some of the "new agenda" issues (e.g., environment, immigration).

As a result of its efforts, the party increased its vote share in three consecutive elections before suffering a minor blow in 2006, while at the same time avoiding isolation (see Table 4.1). Key to this success was the commitment of the membership and the constituencies to the party; in fact, it has been well argued that few organizations can survive very long without loyalty to an organization per se (Orbell and Fougere 1973: 450). The small size of Cyprus definitely played a role in organizational loyalty; smaller states, with a restricted electoral market, have been characterized by dense organizational networks that bond voters into a set of strong identities (Mair 1997: 168).

Nonetheless, the party's substantial electoral strength proved to be a taming influence, causing the party to deemphasize its revolutionary exhortations and concentrate instead on working-class "bread-and-butter issues" and on the improvement of the daily life of those attached to AKEL either directly or indirectly. Practical and everyday politics took precedence over discussions about transforming society, thus avoiding significant internecine disputes over policy questions. The end of the 1980s was a turning point, signalling the beginning of an era in which the party stopped making new demands and focused on defending past achievements (Charalambous 2012b).

AKEL's politics have persuaded the other political forces and various policy-makers that it does not present a threat to liberal democracy but should, rather, be viewed as any other political actor. The fate of the party, however, has relied increasingly on the way its prospects for governing would be treated, given the fact that the influence of ideological objectives were diminishing. In addition, the time lag since the right-wing-led coup of 1974 weakened anti-rightist's feelings among the electorate and threatened to upset the long-lasting frame of political alliances that clearly placed DISY at a disadvantage. AKEL's history of (critically) supporting or indirectly participating in government coalitions and declining to take a negative stance to coalition-building, in contrast to most of its counterparts, was an asset for the party.

NOTE

1. The Cyprus Problem is an unresolved political conflict with two faces: an international side, which refers to the de facto division of the island after the 1974 Turkish invasion, and a bicommunal aspect, which refers to the island's two main ethnicities. The roots of the problem lie during the British colonial period (1878–1960). For details about the Cyprus Problem, see Ker-Lindsay 2011; Mallinson 2010.

BIBLIOGRAPHY

Adams, T. W. (1971). *AKEL: The Communist Party of Cyprus*, California: Hoover Institution Press.

AKEL (1962). *The Programme of AKEL*, Nicosia: AKEL [in Greek].

AKEL (1978). 'The 14th Congress of AKEL', *Neos Democratis*, Issue 54.

AKEL (1986). Proceedings of the 16th Party Congress, Nicosia, 26–30 November.

AKEL (1990) Our Perception of Socialism, Nicosia.

AKEL (1991a). Theseis to the 17th Party Congress, Nicosia, 3–7 October.

AKEL (1991b). Congress' Political Resolution and Other Materials, Nicosia.

AKEL (1991c). 'For Freedom, Democracy and Progress: Our proposal', Nicosia: AKEL [in Greek].

AKEL (1994). 'Proceedings of the Organizational Conference', Nicosia, 11–12 June

AKEL (1995a). Theseis to the 18th Party Congress, Nicosia.

AKEL (1995b). 'Suggestion for reviewing AKEL's position on the issue of Cyprus' Accession to the European Union', Nicosia.

AKEL (1996). Congress' Political Resolution and Other Materials, Nicosia.

AKEL (2000). AKEL's Proposal for the Modernization of Cyprus's Society', Nicosia.

AKEL (2001). Proceedings of the 19th Party Congress, Nicosia, 7–10 December.

AKEL (2005). Theseis to the 20th Party Congress, Nicosia.

AKEL (2006). 'Announcement on the Issue of Cyprus's Entrance in the Eurozone', www.akel.org.cy, retrieved 12 July [in Greek].

AKEL (2007). 'Annual Party Assessment of Organizational Capacity', Nicosia: AKEL

AKEL (2009a). 'Together in Europe as well, Manifesto for the elections of the European Parliament.

AKEL (2009b). Speech in the house of representatives by the party parliamentary spokesman on the ratification of the Treaty of Lisbon.

AKEL (2010a). Report of the Organizational office to the 21st Congress, Nicosia.

AKEL (2010b). Theses of the central committee to the 21st Congress, Nicosia, September.

AKEL (2011a). Statute, Nicosia: AKEL.

AKEL (2015a). Lessons on Marxist Political Economy, Nicosia: AKEL.

AKEL (2015b). Theses of AKEL's Central Committee to the 22nd Congress, Nicosia, 4–7 June, Nicosia: AKEL.

AKEL (2015c). Statute, Nicosia.

Alimi, E., Bosi L., and Demetriou C. (2012). 'Relational Dynamics and Processes of Radicalization: a Comparative Framework', *Mobilization: An International Journal*, 17(1), pp. 7–26

Althusser, L. (1978). 'What must change in the party', *Le Monde* [in four parts on 24, 25, 26, 27 April].

Charalambous, G. (2014). *Political Culture and Behaviour in the Republic of Cyprus during the Crisis*, PCC Report 2/2014, PRIO Cyprus Centre.

Charalambous, G. (2012a). AKEL: A Socio-Political Profile of Greek-Cypriot Communism', In N. Trimikliniotis and U. Bozkurt (Eds) *Beyond a Divided Cyprus: A State and Society in Transformation*, pp. 151–168, Basingstoke: Palgrave Macmillan.

Charalambous, G. (2012b). 'AKEL and the European Union', *Greek Political Science Review*, Issue 38 [in Greek].

Charalambous, G. (2007). 'The Strongest Communists in Europe: Accounting for AKEL's Electoral Success', *Journal of Communist Studies and Transition Politics*, 23 (3), pp. 425–456.

Christophorou, C. (2006). Party Change and Development in Cyprus (1995–2005), *South European Society and Politics*, 11(3–4), pp. 513–542.

Christophorou, C. (2001). Consolidation and Continuity through Change: Parliamentary Elections in Cyprus May 2001', *South European Society and Politics*, 6(2), pp. 97–118.

Dunphy, R., and Bale, T. (2007). 'Red flag still flying?', *Party politics*, 13 (3), pp. 129–146.

Ellinas, A. and Katsourides, Y. (2013). 'Organizational Continuity and Electoral Endurance: the Communist Party of Cyprus', *West European Politics*, 36(4), pp. 859–882

Katsourides, Y. (2014c). 'Partisan Responses to the European Union in Cyprus', *Journal of European Integration*, 36(7), pp. 641–658.

Katsourides, Y. (2014b). 'The National Question in Cyprus and the Cypriot Communist Left in the Era of British Colonialism (1922-1959)', *Journal of Balkan and Near Eastern Studies*, 16(4), pp. 474–501.

Katsourides, Y. (2014a). *The History of the Communist Party in Cyprus: Colonialism, Class and the Cypriot Left*. London: I.B. Tauris.

Katsourides, Y. (2013) 'Determinants of extreme right reappearance in Cyprus: the National Popular Front (ELAM), Golden Dawn's sister party', *South European Society and Politics*, 18(4), pp. 567–589.

Katsourides, Y. (2012). Travelling against the Tide: The Cypriot Communist Left in the Post-1990 Era, *Perspectives on European Politics and Society*, 13 (2), pp. 187–209.

Katsourides, Y. (2003). 'Europeanization and Political Parties in Accession Countries: The Political Parties of Cyprus', Paper Presented at the EpsNet Plenary Conference, Paris, 13–14 June.

Katz, R., and Mair, P. (1995). 'Changing Models of Party Organization: the Emergence of the Cartel Party', *Party Politics*, 1 (1), pp. 5–28.

Ker-Lindsay, J. (2011). *The Cyprus Problem: What Everyone Needs to Know* (Oxford: Oxford University Press).

Ker-Lindsay, J. (2008). Presidential Power and Authority, in Ker-Lindsay, J. and Faustmann, H. (Ed.) *The Government and Politics of Cyprus* (Bern: Peter Lang) pp. 107–124.

Ladrech, R. (2001). 'Europeanization and Political Parties: Towards a Framework of Analysis', Keele European Parties Research Unit (KEPRU), Working Paper 7.

Leventis, G. (2002). *Cyprus: The Struggle for Self-Determination in the 1940s*, Frankfurt am Main: Peter Lang.

Mair, P. (1997). *Party System Change: Approaches and Interpretations*, Oxford: Clarendon Press.

Mallinson, W. (2010). *Cyprus, Diplomatic History and the Clash of Theory in International Relations*, London: I. B. Tauris.

Marioulas, J. (2010). 'The Greek Left', in B. Daiber, Hildebrandt, C. and Striethorst, A. (Eds), *From Revolution to Coalition: Radical Left Parties in Europe*, Berlin: Rosa Luxemburg Stiftung, pp. 292–308.

Orbell, M.J., and Fougere, G. (1973). 'Intra-party Conflict and the Decay of Ideology', *The Journal of Politics*, 35 (2), pp. 439–458

Panayiotou, A. (2014). *The First Left Presidency, 2008-2013*, Limassol: Cyprus Centre for East Mediterranean Studies [in Greek].

Panayiotou, A. (2006). 'Lenin in the Coffee-shop: the Communist Alternative and Forms of non-Western Modernity', *Postcolonial Studies*, 9 (3), pp. 267–280

Peristianis, N. (2006). 'The Rise of the Left and of the Intra-Ethnic Cleavage', in H. Faustmann and N. Peristianis, (Eds), *Britain in Cyprus: Colonialism and Post Colonialism 1878-2006*, Mannheim: Bibliopolis.

PEO (1979). *The Strikes of Miners in 1948*. Nicosia: PEO [in Greek].

Protopapas, V. (2012). *The Electoral History of Cyprus: Politicians, Parties and Elections in Anglokratia 1878–1960*, Athens: Themelio Publications.

Sparsis M. (1998), *Tripartism and Industrial Relations*, Nicosia [in Greek].

Strongos, P. (2010). *Spanish Thermopylae: Cypriot Volunteers in the Spanish Civil War, 1936-39*, London: Tippermuir Books.

CHAPTER 5

The Journey to Power: One Step Forward?

Abstract This chapter analyzes the ways in which AKEL and SYRIZA eventually espoused government participation, emphasizing both the structure of political opportunity and the parties' themselves. The success of these two parties indicates that government participation is increasingly a viable option for RLPs to influence national (and European) politics, as well as a way to remain relevant in the national political and party systems. Analysis reveals how the economic crisis and governing aspirations affected their programs and ideology.

Keywords AKEL • SYRIZA • Government participation • Economic crisis • Memorandum • Cyprus problem • Moderation • Radicalization

The contextual factors that paved the way for the Coalition of the Radical Left (SYRIZA) and the Progressive Party of Working People (AKEL) to make a claim for power were quite different for each party, especially with regard to the economic crisis. When AKEL first made a bid for government office, there was no crisis; local issues predominated, mostly in relation to the long unresolved Cyprus Problem, and the Left's chronic exclusion from government. Because the right and centre-right parties had not been able to solve the island's political problem, many people believed that it was time to give the Left a chance. Moreover, AKEL was at the time rightfully perceived as a party free from scandals and less clientelistic, at least less so than the other parties.

© The Editor(s) (if applicable) and The Author(s) 2016
Y. Katsourides, *Radical Left Parties in Government*,
DOI 10.1057/978-1-137-58841-8_5

In Greece, two factors were critical. First, there was an implosion of the party system—the mismanagement, corruption, and clientelism pervading the system were exposed in 2010 when the Panhellenic Socialist Movement (PASOK) government signed the Memorandum with the Troika. This action discredited the mainstream political actors, especially PASOK, opening a way for new actors to enter (Teperoglou and Tsatsanis 2014). A second important factor was the largely neo-liberal and authoritarian Europeanization process (see Chap. 1), which was widely unpopular among the Greek people and prompted intense reactions. Although the impact of austeritarianism was a compelling factor in the Greek case, it also was a factor that brought the two parties' experiences together.

SYRIZA: THE POLITICAL MOBILIZATION OF ECONOMIC HARDSHIP

SYRIZA's emergence as a governmental actor (Spourdalakis 2013, 2014) and the demise of the social democratic PASOK (Eleftheriou and Tassis 2013; Lamprinou and Balabanidis 2014) heralded party system change in Greece; for the first time in recent Greek political history, a party of (Euro)communist origins successfully established itself as the main representative of the centre-left bloc. SYRIZA's rise was the result of a series of events and processes. A crucial link in this chain of events was definitely the collapse of the Greek party system largely because of the economic crisis; however, another equally important link was SYRIZA's strategy, which clearly understood the changing feelings and demands of the Greek people. This strategy was characterized by an initial phase of radicalization followed by moderation and pragmatism.

SYRIZA's success was clearly somewhat exceptional, with a remarkably favourable combination of external and internal factors. Externally, as Kouvelakis (2011) argued, Greece had undergone an unprecedented, violent socioeconomic change resulting in political polarization. Internally, the "pro-/anti-Memorandum" cleavage sidelined Left–Right ideological debates, discredited the mainstream political parties, gave birth to new party actors, and consolidated contentious practices and discourses in the Greek public sphere. Interrelated was the complete collapse of the mainstream social democratic PASOK because of its role in the imposition of the Troika's policies, as well as its systemic corruption; this allowed SYRIZA to serve as a desirable alternative for disappointed PASOK voters because it was one of the few untainted parties (Tsakatika and Eleftheriou 2013; Eleftheriou 2015). The signing of the Memorandum was the final blow to PASOK's socialist character. PASOK was the first Eurozone government to apply for a loan, insisting that accepting the Memorandum was the only way for Greece to remain in the Eurozone. The austerity measures stipulated in it led to a dramatic deterioration of the economy and caused a deep recession for seven consecutive years (a phenomenon seen previously only in states engaged in warfare), while the Greek public debt as a percentage of GDP rose from 129 % in 2009 to 175 % in 2013 (compared to the EU average of about 90 %). The new policies meant a weakening the trade unions and a reduction of labour costs and public deficits by downsizing the welfare state (Kompsopoulos and Chasoglou 2014: 96; Stavrakakis and Katsambekis 2014: 126); they also led to a redistribution of wealth and power with the upper classes benefiting, the transfer of public services to the private sphere, and the elimination of many fundamental social rights and services (Bournous and Karatsioubanis 2014; Spourdalakis 2013: 105–106).

The violent "proletarianization" of the lower and middle classes created a humanitarian crisis in Greece (Kotsaka and Kotsonopoulos 2012). Unemployment reached 30 % (i.e., 1.6 million people), homelessness and suicide rates snowballed, and one-third of the population lost access to social security and free health care, including children's vaccinations (Laskos and Tsakalotos 2014; Mouriki et al. 2012). The system of governance established in the *Metapolitefsi* could no longer gain legitimation through tax exemptions, job appointments, and other corrupt clientelistic practices. PASOK's support collapsed as a result of policies that severely hurt the classes the party represented. The austerity politics gave rise to numerous movements and resistance groups, as diverse in their composition as in their political goals, and the trade unions held scores of general strikes—27 in total (Kompsopoulos and Chasoglou 2014: 103). Within this context the economic crisis appeared simultaneously as a threefold crisis: representation, legitimization, and responsiveness, thus creating a favourable structure of opportunities for the radical Left (Eleftheriou 2015).

The depth of the crisis shook up traditional partisan attachments. It swept away the entire two-party system of government that had dominated Greece since 1977 and resulted in popular support for parties other than the two main ones (Teperoglou and Tsatsanis 2014). A crisis for the two-party system had been simmering for some time (Spourdalakis 2013: 106).

The ruling parties were gradually becoming delegitimized because they could no longer articulate nor guarantee any kind of "social balance" or "social contract." As explained in Chap. 3, the polarized two-party system of the 1980s gave way to a convergent bipartisanship (Vernardakis 2011), which in turn led to a decisive change in public behaviour. Whereas, during the polarized era, the electoral losses of one party were the gains of the other, and during the consensual period, the decline of the power in one of the two main parties caused a decline in the power of the other. Therefore, it was impossible for the two main parties to absorb the crisis between them and within the traditional framework of alternation in government.

Within this context of a weakened two-party system, many voters sought new political representation and all other political formations became more powerful. Among these, SYRIZA was the most dynamic for two reasons: (1) it had succeeded (and this was a first), through its movement-based radicalism, in surpassing KKE within the Left bloc, as well as becoming the major beneficiary of political protest by a broad social strata; and (2) it benefited from the structural crisis of PASOK by capturing most of its disaffected voters (Tsakatika and Eleftheriou 2013: 13).

Despite the many and very intense ideological positions of the various Greek political parties, the most important political debate was not framed in ideological terms; the classic Left–Right division was replaced by a pro-/anti-Memorandum cleavage (Lyrintzis 2011: 17). This distinction essentially separated the privileged and underprivileged parts of Greek society, cutting across the class divide to forge a political alliance of all those who craved a "change," much as was the case with the PASOK in 1981 (Kotsaka and Kotsonopoulos 2012). The pro-/anti-Memorandum split created such deep divisions between and, sometimes even within, parties that it brought together opponents who ordinarily would never have cooperated—that is, first New Democracy (ND), PASOK, and the Democratic Left (DIMAR); and then SYRIZA and the Independent Greeks (ANEL), a splinter nationalist group from ND. When austerity grew to be an issue of high prominence , ideology became secondary, which enabled groups of voters to change their allegiances more easily than if ideology had been the main issue (Lamprinou and Balabanidis 2014).

In the May and June elections of 2012, the people were filled with anger and disappointment at the mainstream parties; it was their loud call for change that enabled SYRIZA to make a great leap forward. SYRIZA's growing support, from 16.8 % in May to 26.9 % in June, indicated the impressively compressed time frame within which the country's political landscape changed. In less than three years, SYRIZA increased its support fivefold, from 316,000 in October 2009 to 1.7 million in June 2012, and by that time it had emerged as the country's principal opposition force (Voulgaris and Nikolakopoulos 2014; Mavris 2012: 101) (Table 5.1).

SYRIZA's gains, however, cannot be attributed solely to the repercussions of the Memorandum, despite the role these developments played in fueling the radical Left's dynamic rise (Stavrakakis and Katsambekis 2014: 126).

From Protest to Responsible Politics

SYRIZA's rise was neither natural nor deterministic. During periods of great crisis, voter shifts are motivated not only by disillusionment, anxiety, and anger, but also by a party's capacity to offer a different perspective for resolving the crisis. In other European countries the crisis produced completely different political outcomes, confirming the importance of the party's strategy. SYRIZA did not become a major political force in Greece because of its moderate, centrist policy, at least initially; its politics were far more complex than that. The party adopted a radical strategy first, followed by more pragmatic approaches later. The pragmatic shift, according to Moschonas (2015a), was part of SYRIZA's strategy to win the electorate first and push it farther to the Left later. In this process it rapidly transformed from a protest one into a more responsible party; its pragmatism was the result of "maturation" that resulted in transforming SYRIZA into a real government actor.

Table 5.1 The 2012 double elections

Party	May 2012 (%)	June 2012 (%)	Difference (+, −)(%)
ND	18.85	29.66	+10.81
SYRIZA	16.79	26.89	+10.1
Golden Dawn	6.97	6.92	−0.05
KKE	8.48	4.50	−3.98
PASOK	13.18	7.51	−5.67
ANEL	10.65	12.28	+1.63
DIMAR	6.11	6.25	+0.14
Others	18.97	12.24	−12.98

Source: Greek Ministry of Interior

This process of maturation involved three steps (Moschonas 2015a), beginning with intraparty discussion on a possible *Grexit* (i.e., Greece's withdrawal from the Eurozone). Only the minority (i.e., the Left Platform and other components of SYRIZA) supported this view (e.g., see Lapavitsas 2014); the majority (including Tsipras) believed that leaving the Eurozone would only aggravate an already bad situation caused by the Memorandum's austerity policies. The strategy was to seek alliances with the South Europe countries; in other words, SYRIZA intended to Europeanize Greece's problem. Moschonas believes that this discussion was key to SYRIZA's rise, as it enabled the party to expand and refine its program. He argues that the party's initial anti-systemic rhetoric of "protest" and "anti-neo-liberalism" lacked ideological and programmatic depth. Furthermore, the party had no solid proposals for overcoming the debt crisis; it was the intraparty discussion that helped SYRIZA formulate a pragmatic solution.

The party's ability to devise a solution was also facilitated by its commitment to and participation in the European Left (EL) mechanisms and various fora, including the Transform network of research institutes affiliated with EL member and observer parties; most, if not all, of these parties were committed to the euro. The discussions that took (and still are taking) place within these structures enabled the party to consider alternative policy proposals, such as Plan B, and to develop its coalition-building potential with other like-minded parties in Europe (e.g., see Baier 2016). It is evident that SYRIZA both influences and is affected by these discussions. Many of its analyses and slogans conform to EL and Transform texts and resolutions.

The second step involved the party leadership's call to stand in the elections with the goal to become a governing challenger, arguing that the party must do more than simply oppose neo-liberal policies. There were two important implications here: (1) the ranks of SYRIZA supporters swelled, giving the party a strong electoral impetus; (2) the party realized it had to offer realistic solutions to the crisis, taking into consideration people's demands. The third step would be to actually govern (see Chap. 6).

Building on the maturation argument or, alternatively, SYRIZA's social democratization (Tassis and Eleftheriou 2015; Kompsopoulos and Chasoglou 2014: 105), it is possible to identify two phases in SYRIZA's programme and discourse since the onset of the crisis. Initially, from 2010 to 2012, SYRIZA adopted a radical strategy. The party proclaimed that the Memorandum was not simply a technical matter, or an error of judgment by governing parties, but also was the outcome of a global predatory capitalism (Spourdalakis 2013: 109). As such, it should be discarded altogether (Bournous and Karatsioubanis 2014).

SYRIZA's programme and political practice in the early stages aimed to "empower the powerless," as it said. In other words, it was a definite appeal to the losers because of the Memorandum—that is, the wage earners in the public and private sector and the unemployed (Vernardakis 2012). SYRIZA proposed radical reforms, including social control of the banks, higher taxes for the rich, protection of small enterprises, and freezing of privatizations (SYRIZA 2012). The party called for all outstanding loan repayments to be postponed until the economy showed signs of growth, a reorientation of banking activity towards providing credit for development, the abolition of all anti-labor laws, and the reestablishment of many welfare policies (Spyropoulou 2013: 17).

During this period, SYRIZA maintained its already established close ties with social movements and formed many new connections with emerging social and local movements, mainly in urban centres (Tsakiris and Aranitou 2011). Above all, it was SYRIZA's framing of the Greek "Indignants" Movement in 2011 that supplied the party with a mass following and led to explicit demands for democratization; citizen participation; transparency; and, ultimately, electoral success in 2012 (Karamichas 2013; Theodossopoulos 2013). At that time of loud social protest and great political unrest, SYRIZA was the first and probably the only party to engage with the protesters' demands and meet them out in the streets (Stavrakakis and Katsambekis 2014: 126). Many Greeks saw SYRIZA as their party representative in the public sphere and in the parliament.

Spourdalakis (2013: 103) argues that SYRIZA purposively adopted a party model that suited the emerging social developments, which he describes as a "mass connective party." Instead of patronizing the various movements, such as the KKE (Eleftheriou 2015: 63), SYRIZA connected with them in a way that allowed it also to learn from them. This allowed SYRIZA to build a distinct party culture free of inflexible dogmatism and/or the governmentalism of the "moderate" Left (Spourdalakis 2014: 358). SYRIZA's coalitional structure, internal pluralism, and openness provided an organizational locus that was able to easily include new groups, movements, activists, and voters, as well as to adapt to rapid external changes (Tsakatika and Eleftheriou 2013: 14). This strategy also involved participation in all institutions of social and

political representation and the development of a programme that resonated with the people's demands.

Painting a governing profile for the party was the glue that brought
all the various groups together and included, among others, the creation
of a team of technocrats to convey security to the electorate and the
projection of Tsipras as the unifying element of the anti-Memorandum
alliance (Eleftheriou 2015: 65). Tsipras, whom most Greeks viewed as
a young and untainted politician, was pivotal to the positive perception
of SYRIZA and to success. Accordingly, Tsipras developed a Left populist political idiom that reached even right-wing audiences (Stavrakakis
and Katsambekis 2014). His popularity and style of leadership led to his
increased autonomy within the party's organization.

Following the 2012 elections and until the 2015 elections, which the
party won, SYRIZA underwent slow but advancing de-radicalization clearly
associated with its (realistic) government aspirations. To capitalize on the
social protests, the party's discourse became less class-oriented and took
on populist attributes aiming to appeal to larger audiences (Balabanidis
2015a). There were early signs of this transformation in the run-up to the
elections of 17 June 2012, when SYRIZA softened its rhetoric regarding
the Eurozone, as Tsipras publicly declared that it would be foolish to take
the exit route (Dimitrakopoulos 2012: 7). In that extremely uncertain
political landscape between the two elections, SYRIZA tried to win over
more and more undecided voters, and in this effort, it had to mitigate its
radicalism.

Intraparty discussion regarding the issue of government participation was not new. Synaspismos had in fact had two distinct strategies
(Spourdalakis 2014: 356). The modernizers, who left the party to form
DIMAR in 2010, viewed participation in governing institutions as the
sine qua non for a "responsible Left"; a claim that became a self-fulfilling
prophecy, with its participation in Samaras's coalition government with
ND and PASOK, after the June 2012 national elections. The second strategy was based on a different vision and promoted the party's active presence in the social field while pursuing (and later exercising) government
participation. This strategy became politically effective given the social
conditions created by the austerity policies (Eleftheriou et al. 2013); outlined by Dragasakis (2013: 9–43).

Dragasakis (2013) argued that one term in government was not enough
if a strategic transformation was to be effected; however, he warned that
the party members would be ready to resign if necessary. Dragasakis

defined the Memorandum as the political program of domestic political and social elites, not merely a tool of foreign domination; from this it followed that it should be abolished. He prioritized the humanitarian crisis as the central governing challenge, similar to the PCI in the 1970s, and he stressed the importance of stabilizing the economy without loading it with further demands. The primary goal within the extreme conditions provided by the austerity policies was to defend the welfare state and restore some of the rights lost during that period.

After its success in the 2012 elections, SYRIZA had to adjust to its new role as the leading opposition party and as a political power in line to govern. Yet, considering the pressing social conditions and the changing political terrain, SYRIZA found itself once again faced with an old Leninist dilemma: "if not now, then when?" SYRIZA responded with a threefold call that expressed urgent popular demands: (1) eliminate the Memorandum, (2) end "bipartyism," and (3) preserve citizens' dignity (Spourdalakis 2013: 113). It also announced its aim to govern, thus facilitating masses of PASOK voters accustomed to being close to government to switch their vote to SYRIZA. The party's communication strategy accordingly was premised on the potential of the Left government's ability to rule and the shift from an oppositional imaginary to a ruling one. What allowed SYRIZA to jump from a marginal party to one with a very real chance at seizing power seems to be precisely the acceptance of this task of representation (Stavrakakis and Katsambekis 2014: 127). In this process, radical aspirations became secondary and the party emphasized issues of democracy, harshly criticizing the authoritative practices of the ND–PASOK–DIMAR coalition government (Eleftheriou 2015: 67, 70).

The New Narrative of Negotiation

Governing aspirations were not compatible with earlier positions of cancelling the Memoranda that had led to the enormous humanitarian crisis in Greece. Therefore, a new narrative was promoted that emphasized a "negotiation" for a new deal (SYRIZA 2014). This change actually has been endorsed since 2012. Therefore, and without denying earlier analyses of the crisis, SYRIZA changed its strategy. The party decided to draw up a set of policy proposals reflecting a more technocratic and responsible background; and it also decided to prioritize "negotiation" for a new deal rather than clashing with the neo-liberal European and national political elite. Thus, de-radicalization represented the party elite's recognition that traditional opposition tactics could not successfully fight European structures and bureaucracy.

SYRIZA offered only vague indications of an alternative European Union (EU) policy, mainly regarding matters directly involving the Greek debt crisis (e.g., Eurobonds). The party focused more on reintegrating Greece into the European project (SYRIZA 2012: 2). Furthermore, the party announced its plan to carry out the following actions: replace the terms of the Memorandum with plans for social reconstruction, economic restructuring, and fiscal stabilization; build a productive economy through promotion of a new "Marshall Plan"; advocate a debt relief solution (i.e., partial write-off) in the framework of a common EU strategy on the public debt of all member countries; and establish a pan-European mechanism to guarantee bank savings.

Essentially, SYRIZA's strategy was to make Greece's problem an EU problem; therefore, the party demanded that the Greek reform policy be embedded into a European framework in order to achieve mutual strengthening. In January 2013, when the Die Linke and the EL launched their yearly campaign, Tsipras likened Greece to "a laboratory of neoliberal barbarism in Europe" (Tsipras 2013), and called SYRIZA's program a "compass for the European Left and for the entire EU." At the presentation of the economic reform program, the party's MP Dragasakis said: "From the outset we have stated that our programme and our struggle are at the same time both national and European. From the outset we have said that we want to change the blueprint, both for Greece and for Europe" (SYRIZA 2012: 4–5). Therefore, according to Tsipras, Greece should remain within the common currency and on politically equal terms (Synaspismos 2012).

The party also recognized the need to prove its ability to discuss issues with European elites, and after the 2012 elections, Tsipras began to travel throughout Europe and the United States, visiting and speaking at think tanks, giving interviews, and publishing articles in the mainstream international press. This campaign also endeavored to destigmatize the party as an extreme leftist one that would jeopardize the fundamental pillars of the system if elected to government. Tsipras, however, emphasized the need for a new plan to increase European integration, a plan that would challenge neo-liberalism and lead Europe's economies back to recovery by prioritizing the needs of workers, pensioners, and the unemployed over the interests of multinational companies and bankrupt bankers (Tsipras 2012). Tsipras maintained that this was the only way that the EU could restore the European vision of social justice, peace, and solidarity. In this regard, SYRIZA did not completely abandon its leftist rhetoric (Lamprinou and Balabanidis 2014).

Tsipras's political aspirations grew; this was evident in his candidacy for the European Commission in 2014, which also made his claim for the premiership more credible. In response the former Greek government presented him as a far-left, irresponsible politician—a tactic that only served to strengthen Tsipras's popularity, thus further enhancing his autonomy vis-à-vis party organization. Tsipras cleverly recalled memories of the populist 1970s and 1980s by speaking in the name of the "nonprivileged," a highly loaded signifier, which was the main term for the "people" in Andreas Papandreou rhetoric (Stavrakakis and Katsambekis 2014: 128).

The Politics of Hope

Clearly, during this period Greece essentially was divided into two camps: those who were pro- and those who were anti-Memorandum. SYRIZA successfully persuaded all of them on the "losing side" that they would be heard if they trusted the party with their vote. In this phase SYRIZA represented a sort of "left social democracy" with populist and movement characteristics. The party's "social-democratic" politics were quite radical, however, because they went far beyond what was "allowed" and expected within the EU.

SYRIZA realized that should it be voted into government it would face many problems confronting the EU's institutional and political "conservatism" unless it abandoned its left-wing politics. At the same time though, many in the party, acknowledged that "remaining indifferent in the name of a supposed ideological purity or a distorted class prioritization of interests was not an option" (Bournous and Karatsioubanis 2014). They understood that the only way to fight the neo-liberal Memorandum was by means of a policy of alliances aimed at winning the next national elections; a task that the party achieved (Table 5.2).

The 2015 campaign was fought along the lines of continuity versus change, stability versus instability, Euro versus Grexit, austerity versus growth, and fear versus hope (Halikiopoulou and Vasilopoulou 2015). SYRIZA was the advocate of "hope": the party slogan, "Hope is on the way," was accompanied by rhetoric emphasizing a new beginning; justice and equality; an end to the humanitarian crisis created by austerity; a new Europe; and a future with dignity. SYRIZA successfully articulated many

Table 5.2 The 2015 Greek national election results (parties in parliament)

Party	Vote share (%)	Seats
SYRIZA	36.3	149
New Democracy	27.8	76
Golden Dawn	6.3	17
To Potami (The River)	6.1	17
KKE	5.5	15
Independent Greeks	4.8	13
PASOK	4.7	13

Source: Greek Ministry of Interior, http://www.ypes.gr

diffuse demands; its distinct Left Europeanism was key to the party's electoral success. This was because it did not alienate the majority of voters who were angry at the EU for its treatment of Greece but did not want to jeopardize Greece's participation in the EU institutions (Nikolakakis 2015).

Another important feature of SYRIZA's campaign was the active support by the Spanish party, Podemos, which had an anti-austerity agenda similar to SYRIZA's (Tsirbas 2015: 8). This support was expressed in the slogan "SYRIZA-Podemos-Venceremos," as well as by the presence of Podemos's leader, Pablo Iglesias at Tsipras's side, during the main speech made in Athens by the SYRIZA leader three days before the election. In 2015, SYRIZA's main campaign concept, "Hope is coming. Greece moves on—Europe is changing," was intended to portray the party as a changing force for both Greece and Europe. Obviously, the alignment with Podemos served this purpose.

The January 2015 elections that brought SYRIZA into power seem to have reestablished a type of bipartisanship, albeit a weaker version overall. The new constellation of parties also appeared to conform to traditional Greek political standards (Kiapidou 2015a) with PASOK, at one time the ND's strongest opponent, replaced by SYRIZA. Simultaneously, the crisis also brought an important change to Greek politics: from absolute majority single-party government to coalition formation. The day after the election SYRIZA immediately formed a coalition government with ANEL, a right-wing nationalist party—an act seen by many as ideologically inconsistent. In actual fact it was not surprising because both parties had earlier expressed their willingness to cooperate should SYRIZA not reach the 151 seats required by the Greek constitution for a single-party government.

SYRIZA's election to government represented the first major challenge to austerity politics in Europe, and a milestone for the European Left insofar as it led many to wonder whether it might cause a domino effect in other European countries. SYRIZA's win marked a popular will for a total change of the governing paradigm and economic policies (Tsirbas 2015). In its effort to secure executive power, however, SYRIZA had traveled a long distance, of course, from early 2012 to early 2015; during the process, diluting its political position on a variety of issues, toning down some of its slogans, downplaying the more radical elements of its policy proposals, and shelving some altogether in the context of a general drift to the centre-right.

Some social analysts consider SYRIZA "populist," correctly pointing out the demagogic aspects of its discourse (Stavrakakis and Katsambekis 2014). Others believe that SYRIZA's continuing link with Marxism, its anti-nationalist culture, its immigration policy, and its anti-hierarchical organizational model are all important factors working against its transformation into a populist party of the Left (Moschonas 2015a). For all its momentum, in 2015, SYRIZA was still a new party, lacking both cohesion and programmatic clarity that would allow the party to confront the European elites.

AKEL: Claiming Its Share in Power and Policy-Making

In his study of 34 nonruling communist parties worldwide, Rice (1973: 607) identified AKEL as one of the likely exceptions to an otherwise strong projection that most legal communist parties had no prospect of gaining power either alone or in coalition with other parties. His prediction was realized 35 years later, when AKEL became the first communist party to govern an EU member state. The local conditions leading to AKEL's achievement were significantly different compared to the conditions in Greece responsible for SYRIZA's rise to power. AKEL's hold of the executive position was essentially because of national circumstances, particularly Cyprus's unresolved political problem, but also the party's continued exclusion from higher state office despite its commitment to liberal democracy and its establishment as a "normal" political actor.

AKEL had successfully survived a first challenge—the dissolution of the socialist bloc—and in the early 2000s faced a second important challenge when it turned from defensive strategies to offensive ones in its aspiration to govern. This strategy was not a new idea; in 1995, in addition to changing its stance on joining the EU, the party declared power-sharing as the guiding principle of any future alliance (AKEL 1995a: 16). AKEL's strategy in local politics was similar to its position on the EU: "fighting the system from within." This meant that AKEL accepted the need to work within bourgeois institutions in order to transform them; and it was not a new stance, as it had essentially operated since the 1940s. This strategy was typical of the party's chronic pragmatism (Dunphy and Bale 2007; Christophorou 2006; Panayiotou 2006) and not the result of an ideological debate. Pragmatism was also evident in the party's increasing emphasis on electioneering.

The party's pragmatic acceptance of participation in governing institutions was never complemented by a rigorous analysis of state power, especially in terms of how this differed from participation in governing institutions. State power was, therefore, very simplistically interpreted as a tool for improving the popular strata's working and living conditions and was never associated with any long-term plan for socialism.

AKEL always focused on coming to power in a peaceful, electoral way by forming strategic alliances; this strategy conforms to the Leninist stages of struggle and the party's understanding that social and political conditions had to be right before a communist candidate could run for the presidency (Kolokasides 2010). In this regard, the party prioritized the solution of the Cyprus problem and reunification of the country—what it called the first stage of the struggle (i.e., stage of liberation) (AKEL 2000: 27, 42). Throughout these years the party pursued a strategy of "creative nonparticipation," and therefore offered critical support to centrist candidates without assuming any government office itself until 2003. The loss of the 1993 and 1998 presidential elections to the DISY candidate represented the low point in the party's influence on decision making (Dunphy and Bale 2007: 137); at the same time, these losses resulted in the party taking a more aggressive approach towards office-seeking. This meant that more compromises were necessary.

To understand AKEL's rise in government in 2008, it is necessary to first look at the history of the party's dealings with institutions of governance. In so doing, we notice that prior to the island's independence in 1960 and in the absence of indigenous political institutions, the Church of Cyprus constituted the principal locus of power in the Greek community (Sant Cassia 1986: 5–15). Consequently, and although a communist party, AKEL involved itself in all intra-Church elections, which it saw as a means to influence power and policy-making; this also was indicative of its pragmatism (Katsiaounis 2000).

Cyprus's independence in 1960 marked both the country's inclusion in the Western bloc and the hegemony of right-wing forces in the new state, which was heavily populated by the former National Organisation of Cypriot Fighters (EOKA) and sympathizers (Christophorou and Xadjikiriakos 1996: 3). In the first presidential elections AKEL supported an independent candidate (I. Clerides) against the popular anti-colonial struggle leader, Archbishop Makarios. Clerides polled approximately one-third of the votes; this was the beginning of many years of an AKEL strategy that meant not claiming power with party candidates, but instead supporting centre-right or centre-left personalities. This strategy was dictated by the need to acquire political allies beyond the Left.

Makarios, although an opponent in 1960, turned out to be one such ally. Having realized that socialism was not an achievable goal, AKEL adopted a policy of unity and offered its support to Makarios and his goal of securing Cyprus's independence. This strategy enabled the Cypriot Left to have an important say in the creation of Cyprus's welfare state and also in the decision for a multipolar foreign policy not bound to the Western frame (Panayiotou 2014: 11).

AKEL continued to advocate this strategy and supported a number of centre-right governments until 1985. At that time the party had a serious disagreement with the centre-right DIKO and then President Spyros Kyprianou over the Cyprus Problem. Consequently, AKEL backed G. Vassiliou who, although not a party member per se, had firm leftist (family) origins. Because of his middle-class status as an entrepreneur, Vassiliou was accepted by many beyond the Left, and he won the presidential election in 1988. AKEL participated in the cabinet with two nonparty members.

Although Vassiliou failed in his bid for reelection in 1993, his presidency was positively perceived and left a progressive mark on Cyprus's politics. During his tenure the first local university was established, a number of secular practices were put in place (e.g., civil divorce), the monopoly of the Right in the civil service was terminated, and the Cyprus Problem came closer to a solution as never before. As a result of the Vassiliou and AKEL loss in the 1993 presidential election, for the next decade the Cypriot Right governed the country either alone or in cooperation with the centre-right DIKO or the centre-left EDEK.

AKEL's earlier decision to reposition the party by making changes to its organization, ideology, and program (see Chap. 4) succeeded in making it a potential legitimate governing partner. Signs of this strategy's success can be seen first in 1996 when AKEL partnered with EDEK in municipal elections, and then once again in 1998 when it joined forces with DIKO in the presidential elections. Then, in the 2001 and 2006 local elections, the party formed a three-party coalition to win most of the municipalities. It was in the 2003 presidential elections, however, that the party truly achieved democratic legitimacy (for the concept see Bosco 2001: 333).

In 2003 AKEL formed a coalition with EDEK and DIKO (headed by T. Papadopoulos) in a bid for the presidency for the Republic. The coalition's bid was successful, so Papadopoulos was elected president (2003–2008) and the AKEL party was rewarded with four ministerial appointments. This was the first time the party had participated in the cabinet and represented two important achievements. First, it indicated that the party successfully made a first step towards taking power in its own right (AKEL 2005: 25); second, it revealed an important change to the structure of party competition in Cyprus. AKEL suffered under Cyprus's closed-party system—a system in which governing alternatives and patterns of alternation were established, which led to some parties being regularly excluded from an executive role (Mair 1997: 191). In Cyprus the Left was traditionally excluded, and AKEL was treated as an outsider.

Although the party enjoyed the usual benefits associated with office, it also suffered criticism for failing to deliver on its promises. The grievances were exacerbated after the referendum in April 2004, when Greek Cypriots rejected the UN plan for a solution of the Cyprus Problem as unjust and biased towards the Turkish side. The new historical context of the problem, as reshaped in the Annan Plan and post-Annan Plan, which saw a socially dividing campaign around it, exposed an additional underlying reason for social and political antagonism. This essentially involved those, including the president at the time Papadopoulos and the centre parties supporting him (i.e., DIKO, EDEK, and the Ecologists), who called for a rejection of the Plan; those who called for a positive vote (i.e., DISY); and those who were unsure but eventually tilted towards a "soft no" (i.e., AKEL).

The referendum divided party members and supporters, with the decision reluctantly made to recommend a "no" vote, endorsed by a 65–35 % conference vote (*Haravgi*, 15 April 2004). The effect of this decision was reflected in the European Parliament elections held one month later, where AKEL's percentage shrank to 27.89 % and lagged behind the DISY. It was the party's first real reversal since 1990 and was repeated in the 2006 parliamentary elections with the party's vote share slipping by 3.6 % (Table 5.3).

Anticipation over forthcoming elections always referred back to governmental politics (Laver 2008: 534). AKEL's decision to field its leader as a candidate and thus break its own tradition seemed, in part, to reflect that principle. There was dissatisfaction over a variety of concerns: the Cyprus Problem, the party fortunes under a second Papadopoulos government, how to regain votes lost because of the negative stance on the referendum, and the lack of benefits for social groups represented by the party. The split caused by the 2004 referendum had a significant impact on AKEL's policy of alliances. Many party members and much of the leadership believed that the party should no longer support other party candidates but, rather, claim power on its own.

Therefore, in an effort to allay future electoral damage AKEL announced its presidential aspirations (AKEL 2005: 56), stating that the time was ripe to reverse its traditional policy of alliances and put forth its leader to head a government coalition (Kolokasides 2010: 151). Moreover, opinion polls at that time revealed AKEL's leader, D. Christofias, as the most popular one in the country, and the person with the best chance of solving the Cyprus Problem. The Republic of Cyprus was under increased international and EU pressure because of its rejection of the UN-sponsored plan to solve the problem, and Christofias candidacy was believed to be a way out from this. That fact, together with the strong economy in Cyprus, encouraged party ambitions, confirming the importance of the domestic context and local conditions over any internationalist preoccupations.

Table 5.3 AKEL's National (N) and European (E) election results, 2001–2011

Election year	Percentage	Votes	Seats
2001 (N)	34.71	142,648	20
2004 (E)	27.89	93,212	2
2006 (N)	31.13	131,066	18
2009 (E)	34.90	106,922	2
2011 (N)	32.67	132,163	19

Source: Cyprus Ministry of Interior

AKEL also considered that having its own candidate run for president was a way to end the party's ostracism within the political system and to acquire acceptance as a legitimate democratic actor. As such, it was also a claim for democratization (Panayiotou 2014), a goal the party consistently pursued in various forms and fields. It is in that context that we can find at least a partial explanation for AKEL's policy of cooperation with other political parties (Panayiotou 2014); these alliances allowed the party to push for further democratization of the anti-communist state machinery.

In May–June 2007, the party initiated in-house discussions with party cells to consider the presidential bid; this consultative vote led to a party congress in July 2007 for a decision to be made. Christofias's candidacy was supported during the consultative phase by 80 % of the party membership and 85 members of the 100-member central committee. The congress endorsed his candidacy with 92.7 % in favour (Katsourides 2012: 200). During the campaign it became obvious that his nomination served as a way to revive the party organizationally and programmatically. In this regard, the party candidacy was the choice most suited for avoiding an exchange between votes and policy-making (Charalambous 2009: 103). First, his candidacy would win back those voters who had left the party when it rejected the Annan Plan; and second, the party would be able to pursue its own policies, especially with regard to the Cyprus Problem.

Underlying the presidential bid, and the electoral program proposed, was the party's firm belief that "governing must be pursued even if the preconditions for the implementation of a socialist programme do not exist" (Kolokasides 2010: 149). AKEL saw its bid for the presidency as way to finally have a share in state power and a way to play a powerful role in policy-making. Systemic change, and/or an attempt to change Cyprus into a more socialist country, were not part of the plan. Thus, first and foremost, Christofias presented himself as the candidate who could finally solve the Cyprus Problem. Finally, and very importantly, they proposed a mixed economy to appease any concerns among business circles (Christofias 2007a: 39).

Past participation in government and future expectations further influenced party positioning on European integration and internal affairs. Although EU issues never proved decisive in elections, AKEL's cautious stance towards it was thought to be a point of weakness, so the party toned down its radicalism on EU-related issues during the 2008 presidential campaign in an effort to defuse its salience in political debates

(Katsourides 2014c). Similarly, the party positions on internal government affairs did not go beyond the existing capitalist system, although they were directed in favour of the popular strata interests. This was sufficient for a successful campaign, but it placed the party's identity at risk, as exemplified by a statement by Christofias that, if elected, the party and the president would only "administer the capitalist system" (Christofias 2007b: 23, 31).

Although some believed that AKEL did not differ significantly from other political parties, it nevertheless represented an untested political force. At the same time many acknowledged that it was an alternative to nationalism, neo-liberalism, and one-dimensional geopolitical orientation towards the West. Prioritizing the Cyprus Problem proved an effective way to avoid radical proposals and confrontational strategies and to encourage more consensual approaches. Nevertheless, the Christofias campaign for a "fairer society" generated enormous expectations around social issues, even well beyond AKEL's constituency, which backfired for the party, especially when the economic crisis broke out (see Chap. 6).

Christofias was elected in the runoff after securing the support of the centre-right DIKO and the social democratic EDEK. His election was positively welcomed not only in Cyprus but also by foreign governments, particularly because it was anticipated that he would eventually solve the Cyprus Problem—this was expected because of another circumstance. When Christofias assumed office, the leader of the Turkish Cypriot community was Mehmet Ali Talat, also a leftist and leader of the centre-left Republican Turkish Party (CTP) with which AKEL had had a long-term close relationship. Talat was a known supporter of a solution, and it was believed that the timing was right to resolve the Cyprus Problem.

Still, the most significant aspect of Christofias's election was probably the fact that he claimed power in the name of an entire political space, the Left, which had hitherto been excluded (Panayiotou 2014: 39). Essentially, it represented the demand for government participation by the lower social strata that had always been excluded because of class and ideological discrimination; however, it probably was also a demand to take part in the benefits associated with governing (e.g., clientelism). A largely overlooked issue at the time was Christofias's election as a much-anticipated test of a radical Left party's ability to govern. Governmental power, especially through a party leader, was also a high-risk stake because it involved jeopardizing the party's most valuable asset—AKEL was the only party in Cyprus unaffected by government spoils.

BIBLIOGRAPHY

AKEL (1995a). Theseis to the 18th Party Congress, Nicosia.

AKEL (2000). AKEL's Proposal for the Modernization of Cyprus's Society', Nicosia.

AKEL (2005). Theseis to the 20th Party Congress, Nicosia.

Baier, W. (2016). 'Europe's Left on its Way to Readjusting its European Strategy', On the Conferences in Paris, Berlin, Madrid, Brussels and Athens, http://www.transform-network.net/en/blog/blog-2016/news/detail/Blog/europes-left-on-its-way-to-redefining-its-european-policy.html, accessed 24 March 2016.

Balabanidis, Y. (2015a). 'Radical Left, the Heir of Many Ancestors', Sygxrona Themata, 130–131 (December), pp. 46–50 [in Greek].

Bosco, A. (2001). 'Four Actors in Search of a Role: The Southern European Communist Parties', in N. Diamandouros and R. Gunther (Eds), Parties, Politics and Democracy in the New Europe, Baltimore: John Hopkins University Press.

Bournous, Y. and Karatsioubanis, Y. (2014). 'Austerity, Collapse, and the Rise of the Radical Left in Greece', New Politics, XV(2), http://newpol.org/content/austerity-collapse-and-%E2%80%A8rise-radical-left-greece, Accessed 15 May 2015.

Charalambous, G. (2009). 'The February 2008 Presidential Election in the Republic of Cyprus: The Context, Dynamics and Outcome in Perspective', The Cyprus Review, 21(1), pp. 97–122.

Christofias, D. (2007a). 'Campaign Manifesto', Nicosia: AKEL.

Christofias, D. (2007b). 'Questions and Answers', Nicosia: AKEL.

Christophorou, C. (2006). Party Change and Development in Cyprus (1995–2005), South European Society and Politics, 11(3–4), pp. 513–542.

Christophorou, C. and Xadjikiriakos, A. (1996). Parliamentary Elections: History, Numbers, Analysis, Nicosia: Intercollege Press.

Dimitrakopoulos, D. (2012). 'The Greek Elections of 2012 and Greece's Future in the Eurozone', Swedish Institute for European Policy Studies, European Policy Analysis 2012: 7, pp. 1–8, available at www.sieps.se.

Dragasakis, Y. (2013). 'From the Memoranda to the Reconstruction and Radical Transformation of Greek Society', in C. Kefalis (Ed.) Government of the Left: Way Forward or Parenthesis?, Athens: Topos, pp. 9–43 [in Greek].

Dunphy, R., and Bale, T. (2007). 'Red flag still flying?', Party politics, 13 (3), pp. 129–146.

Eleftheriou, C. (2015). 'The Greek Radical Left and the Crisis (2010-2015): Aspects of a Great Overturn', Sygxrona Themata, 130–131, December, pp. 61–73 [in Greek].

Eleftheriou, C. and Tassis, Ch. (2013). PASOK: The Rise and Fall of a Hegemonic Party, Athens: Savallas [in Greek].

Eleftheriou, C., Spourdalakis, M. and Tsakiris, A. (2013), 'Greek radical left reactions against the crisis: three types of political mobilization, one beneficiary', paper presented at the conference 'The radical left and crisis in Europe: From marginality to the mainstream?' University of Edinburgh, Edinburgh, UK, 17 May.

Halikiopoulou, D. and Vasilopoulou, S. (2015). 'The middle class is the key to retaining power', in R. Gerodimos (Eds), *First thoughts on the 25 January 2015 election in Greece*, GPSG Pamphlet No 4, Published on 2 February 2015 by the Greek Politics Specialist Group (GPSG).

Karamichas, J., (2013), 'Challenges of Researching the Indignants (Aganaktismenoi) of Athens, Greece', *CritCom* available at: http://councilforeuropeanstudies. org/critcom/challenges-of-researching-the-indignants-aganaktismenoi-of-athens-greece-online/.

Katsiaounis, R. (2000). *The Constitutional Treaty of 1946–48*, Nicosia: Cyprus Research Centre. [in Greek].

Katsourides, Y. (2014a). *The History of the Communist Party in Cyprus: Colonialism, Class and the Cypriot Left*. London: I.B. Tauris.

Katsourides, Y. (2012). Travelling against the Tide: The Cypriot Communist Left in the Post-1990 Era, *Perspectives on European Politics and Society*, 13 (2), pp. 187–209.

Kiapidou, N. (2015a). 'What has been the impact of the Eurozone Crisis on the Greek Party System: Evidence from the 2015 Greek National Election', https://epern.wordpress.com/2015/02/02/what-has-been-the-impact-of-the-eurozone-crisis-on-the-greek-party-system-evidence-from-the-2015-greek-national-election/, accessed 10 February 2015.

Kolokasides, Y. (2010). The Left in Government: the Case of Cyprus', in B. Daiber (Ed.) *The Left in Government*, Brussels: Rosa Luxembourg Foundation, pp. 149–156.

Kompsopoulos, J. and Chasoglou, J. (2014). 'The Collapse and Transformation of the Greek Party System', *Socialism and Democracy*, 28(1), pp. 90–112.

Kotsaka, T. and Kotsonopoulos, L. (2012). 'From Crisis to Crisis: State policies and the formation of hegemonic socio-political blocs in the context of inverted democratization', Paper produced for the first phase of the Project: *Austerity policies and political representation crisis: New challenges for the Southern European Left*, Nicos Poulantzas Institute, Athens.

Kouvelakis, S. (2011). 'The Greek Cauldron', *New Left Review*, 72, pp. 17–32.

Lamprinou, K. and Balabanidis, Y. (2014). 'The unstable transformation of the Greek centre – left – From the elections of 2009 to the elections of 2012', in Voulgaris, Y. and Nikolakopoulos E. (Eds) *2012: The Double Earthquake*, pp. 125–150, Athens: Themelio [In Greek].

Laskos, Ch. and Tsakalotos, E. (2014). *Crucible of Resistance: Greece, the Eurozone and the World Economic Crisis*, London: Pluto Press.

Lapavitsas, C. (2014). *A Radical Programme for Greece and the Periphery of the Eurozone*, Athens: Livanis [in Greek].

Laver, M. (2008). 'Governmental Politics and the Dynamics of Multiparty Competition', *Political Research Quarterly*, 61(3), pp. 532–536.

Lyrintzis, C. (2011). 'Greek Politics in the Era of Economic Crisis: Reassessing Causes and Effects', Hellenic Observatory Papers on Greece and Southeast Europe, 45.

Mair, P. (1997). *Party System Change: Approaches and Interpretations*, Oxford: Clarendon Press.

Mavris, Y. (2012), 'Greece's Austerity Election, *New Left Review*,76, pp. 95–107.

Moschonas, G. (2015a). 'Syriza's Tremendous Path to Power', http://www.versobooks.com/blogs/1834-gerassimos-moschonas-syriza-s-tremendous-path-to-power, accessed 3 February 2015.

Muriki, A., Mpalourdos, D. And Papaliou, O. (Eds) (2012). *The Social Portrait of Greece 2012: Aspects of the Crisis*, Athens: EKKE [in Greek].

Nikolakakis, N. (2015). 'The historic victory of Syriza's Left Europeanism', in R. Gerodimos (Eds), First thoughts on the 25 January 2015 election in Greece, GPSG Pamphlet No 4, Published on 2 February 2015 by the Greek Politics Specialist Group (GPSG).

Panayiotou, A. (2014). *The First Left Presidency, 2008-2013*, Limassol: Cyprus Centre for East Mediterranean Studies [in Greek].

Panayiotou, A. (2006). 'Lenin in the Coffee-shop: the Communist Alternative and Forms of non-Western Modernity', *Postcolonial Studies*, 9 (3), pp. 267–280

Rice, G. (1973). 'The Electoral Prospects for Non-ruling Communist Parties', American Journal for Political Science, 17 (3), pp. 597–610.

Sant Cassia, P. (1986). 'Religion, Politics and Ethnicity in Cyprus during the Turkocratia (1571– 1878)', *European Journal of Sociology*, 27(1), pp. 3–28.

Spourdalakis, M. (2014), 'The Miraculous Rise of the 'Phenomenon SYRIZA''', *International Critical Thought*, 4(3), pp. 354–366.

Spourdalakis, M. (2013), 'Left Strategy in the Greek Cauldron: Explaining SYRIZA's Success', in L. Panitch, G. Albo and V. Chibber (Eds), *Socialist Register 2013: The Question of Strategy*, London: Merlin Press, pp. 98–120.

Spyropoulou, V. (2013). 'Hard Times to Win: Explaining the Rise of the Radical Left in the Last Elections in Greece', Paper presented at the ECPR General Conference, Bordeaux, 4–7 September.

Stavrakakis, Y. and Katsambekis, G. (2014). 'Left-wing Populism in the European Periphery: the case of Syriza', *Journal of Political Ideologies*, 19(2), pp. 119–142.

Synaspismos (2012). Speech of Alexis Tsipras, President of SYRIZA, during the presentation of the party programme, 1 June 1, www.syn.gr/gr/keimeno.php?id=27330.

SYRIZA (2014). 'The Thessaloniki Programme', http://www.syriza.gr/article/id/57965/OMILIA-TOY-PROEDROY-TOY-SYRIZA-ALEKSH-TSIPRA-STO-SYNEDRIAKO-KENTRO-I.-BELLIDHS-ThESSALONIKH-13-9-2014.html#.VnrVX8tukdU, Accessed 15 September 2014.

SYRIZA (2012). The Economic Programme of SYRIZA-USF (Coalition of Radical Left – United Social Front): www.syriza.gr/the-economic-programme-ofsyriza-usf-coalition-of-radical-left-united-social-front.

Tassis, C. and Eleftheriou, C. (2015). 'The Pasokification of SYRIZA: Towards a Change of Paradigm?', http://www.efsyn.gr/arthro/h-pasokopoiisi-toy-syriza-proaggelos-gia-allagi-politikoy-paradeigmatos, accessed 27 August 2015.

Teperoglou, E. and Tsatsanis, E. (2014), 'Dealignment, Delegitimation and the Implosion of the Two-Party System in Greece: The Earthquake Election of 6 May 2012', *Journal of Elections, Public Opinion and Parties*, 24(2), pp. 222–242.

Theodossopoulos, D. (2013), 'Infuriated with the Infuriated? Blaming Tactics and Discontent about the Greek Financial Crisis', *Current Anthropology*, 54(2), pp. 200–221.

Tsakatika, M. and Eleftheriou, C. (2013), 'The Radical Left's Turn towards Civil Society in Greece: One Strategy, Two Paths', *South European Society and Politics*, 18(1), pp. 81–99.

Tsakiris, A. and Aranitou, V. (2011). 'Can't pay? Don't pay!: Civil Disobedience Movements and Social Protest in Greece during the Memorandum Era, paper presented at the 16th Alternative Futures and Popular Protest Conference, Manchester, 18–20 April.

Tsipras, A. (2013). 'Greece could be the spark for defeating austerity across Europe', *The Guardian*, www.guardian.co.uk/commentisfree/video/2013/mar/19/alexis-tsipras-syriza-greece-video-interview, accessed 22 August 2015.

Tsipras, A. (2012). 'The Greek message for Angela Merkel', *The Guardian*, October 8, www.guardian.co.uk/commentisfree/2012/oct/08/greek-messagefor-angela-merkel, accessed 5 September 2015.

Tsirbas, Y. (2015). 'The January 2015 Parliamentary Election in Greece: Government Change, Partial Punishment and Hesitant Stabilization', *South European Society and Politics*, http://dx.doi.org/10.1080/13608746.2015.1088428.

Vernardakis, C. (2012). The June 17th elections and the new cleavages in the Greek party system, Avgi [Dawn], 24 June [in Greek].

Vernardakis, C. (2011). *Political Parties, Elections and the Party System: The Transformations of Political Representation 1990-2010*, Athens: Sakkoulas [in Greek].

Voulgaris, Y. and Nikolakopoulos, E. (2014). 'Introduction: The Electoral Earthquake of 2012, in Y. Voulgaris and E. Nikolakopoulos (Eds), *2012: The Twin Earthquake Elections*, Athens: Themelio, pp. 9–31 [in Greek].

CHAPTER 6

The Radical Left in Government: Two Steps Back

Abstract This chapter analyzes the AKEL and the SYRIZA trajectories as governing parties and emphasizes the impact of government-opposition dynamics on their ideological and political positions. It is argued that both parties have been reluctant to launch radical proposals or solutions consistent with their ideology and their past. Endorsing a long-term vision for radical social change, as well as their traditional anti-capitalist positions, while governing in the EU context, seems a mission (almost) impossible. This balancing act can at times lead to intraparty tensions.

Keywords AKEL • SYRIZA • Government participation • Economic crisis • Moderation • Radicalization • Inexperience • Party and government

Radical Left parties (RLPs) rarely have found themselves in a governing position. Even when this has occurred they were junior coalition partners to big social democratic parties (Olsen et al. 2010). Nonetheless, this is changing, at least in some countries; for example, in Greece, the Coalition of the Radical Left (SYRIZA), and Cyprus, the Progressive Party of Working People (AKEL), where the parties were elected to govern as senior partners in coalition governments. This chapter contains an overview their course while in government and indirectly engages with the broader question of what to expect when left-wing radicals achieve governance. This question is now of particular importance given the emergence

© The Editor(s) (if applicable) and The Author(s) 2016   117
Y. Katsourides, *Radical Left Parties in Government*,
DOI 10.1057/978-1-137-58841-8_6

of radical leftists in other parts of Europe (e.g., Corbyn in the United Kingdom and Podemos in Spain). Considering that neo-liberalism appears to predominate in European Union (EU) structures, as well as in its governing bodies and policies (Bruff 2014; Schmidt and Thatcher 2014), we must wonder whether RLPs can pursue their principles of fundamental societal change when they are in government or whether they become embedded within the very system they were set to change.

SYRIZA in Government: From Marx to Keynes and Beyond

Minutes after being sworn in as the first leftist Prime Minister of Greece, Alexis Tsipras visited the National Resistance Memorial in Kaisariani and laid flowers in memory of the 200 communists who were executed by the Nazis on May Day 1944. It was a symbolic act with two main objectives. First, he aimed to show his intention of resisting the German call for austerity politics in Greece, thus conveying the message to the Greek people that he would fight to restore "their lost dignity." Second, he meant to specifically target the Greek leftists who—widely persecuted after their defeat in the 1946–1949 bloody civil war—would find such a gesture hugely significant. Before visiting Kaisariani he also had broken with tradition by not being sworn in by the head of Greece's Orthodox Church, Archbishop Ieronymos.

Although symbolism in politics matters greatly, real life and real politics matter more, especially in the long run. Post-election, SYRIZA's politics have given rise to much criticism. At the heart of this criticism were three issues: (1) the cooperation with the nationalist Independent Greeks (ANEL) party; (2) the election of rightist P. Pavlopoulos as President of the Republic; and, above all, (3) their acceptance of neo-liberal politics initiated by the initial agreement (21 February) signed with the Eurogroup that culminated in the third Memorandum voted on by the Greek parliament on 14 August 2015. The last act initiated a process of rapid party transformation and de-radicalization, which led to intense internal strife and placed the party at the epicentre of passionate criticism from various leftist parties and organizations as well as opposition parties.

Both for analytical reasons and because of internal (party) changes, SYRIZA's experience in government will be broken down in two phases. The initial phase covers the period of the first SYRIZA government (January–September 2015), when the party lost its majority in parliament after several party MPs questioned the Prime Minister's policies, particularly the signing of the third Memorandum. As a result, Tsipras resorted to new elections in September 2015, which initiated the second phase of the party's government.

Strange Bedfellows and Other Choices

The first act of the radical Left government that prompted reaction was their cooperation with ANEL, a splinter group from *Nea Dimokratia* and a nationalist, authoritarian, populist right-wing party (Halikiopoulou and Vasilopoulou 2015). This party's motto, "motherland, religion and family," fundamentally contradicts SYRIZA's left-wing, socially open ideals (e.g., their pro-immigration stance and call for the separation of church and state). This indicates that there is a chasm separating SYRIZA and ANEL on the Green-Alternative-Libertarian (GAL) versus the Traditional-Authoritarian-Nationalist (TAN) axis (Andreadis 2015) and has led some scholars to brand this coalition as "unholy" (Balabanidis 2015a: 48).

A few years ago no one could imagine that parties so distant on the ideological spectrum would even discuss such a negotiation. In 2012, the SYRIZA EMP, Papadimoulis, tweeted that a government opposing the Memorandum's austerity politics could never work with the participation of ANEL and its leader, P. Kammenos, because the party and its leader were to the right of ND. Less than three years later, however, what seemed inconceivable became fact. Astonishingly, what united SYRIZA and ANEL was their anti-austerity stance. Because the Greek Communist Party (KKE) had explicitly ruled out cooperation with SYRIZA, the only possible partner left for it in the anti-Memorandum camp was ANEL (Tsirbas 2015: 5). Therefore, strategy rather than ideology guided their coalition. Their cooperation also was aided by the decline of the Left–Right cleavage and the rise of other forms of division such as Troika versus anti-Troika, new versus old, and so on (Teperoglou 2015).

From its perspective it was also important to cooperate with a political party that would have a strong foothold in areas where SYRIZA's ministers would be at least uneasy and almost definitely inefficient—areas crucial for the proper functioning of the country such as the police and, especially, the army (Gkasis 2015). Moreover, SYRIZA wanted to avoid extreme ideological associations. Had SYRIZA governed alone the conflict would have become an ideological battle instead of a pro-/anti-Memorandum conflict, which resonated better with the electorate.

During the first months in power, government rhetoric focused less on class in favour of a more "national rhetoric," thus highlighting the danger of undermining SYRIZA's radical profile (Sevastakis 2015: 30; Papadopoulou and Spourdalakis 2015). In addition, Tsipras's decision to appoint ANEL leader, P. Kammenos, as Minister of Defence raised questions about the future of foreign policy and the so-called "national questions." The preceding created conditions of intraparty tumult from the very beginning. SYRIZA's radical factions, which then included Trotskyist, Maoist, and Stalinist groups, reacted to this cooperation; this only aggravated the problem and made the new government extremely fragile from the start, with a small margin for losses.

Within the first month of SYRIZA's governing tenure another test of its leftism emerged with the election of the new President of the Republic. SYRIZA deliberately backed P. Pavlopoulos, a well-known rightist, former MP, and minister of *Nea Dimokratia*. His candidacy was put forward in a bid to bring the cross-party support needed to renegotiate a new deal with Greece's international creditors and to bolster the leftist government in its critical EU bailout talks. The government's choice puzzled some within the party (e.g., MP Lapavitsas 2015), as Pavlopoulos's legacy was inconsistent with the new radical Left government's pledges to revolutionize political life in the country.

Criticism focused on a number of issues concerning Pavlopoulos's past; for example, clientelistic practices in favour of rightists and his alleged role in the fatal police shooting of a 15-year-old Greek student, A. Grigoropoulos, and the riots that broke out afterwards. Tsipras justified his choice arguing that the new president had "a proven democratic sensitivity, a strong national conscience, and broad approval in society and parliament."[1]

(Soft) Neo-liberal Convergence

For a newcomer party (i.e., SYRIZA), which had never undergone the test of power, the victory in January 2015 highlighted how five years of fiscal orthodoxy in Europe, and particularly in Greece, had turned politics upside down. "For the first time a 'child' of the European crisis, an explicitly anti-austerity party, took office in the EU" (Traynor 2015). SYRIZA won office because it promised to put an end to Greece's submission to the rule of the Troika.

As such, its victory was presented as the biggest challenge to the era of "There Is No Alternative" (TINA) and signalled the reemergence of the Left as a political force; many anticipated the launch of a radical alternative. Greece no longer was viewed as a social laboratory for testing the most extreme neo-liberal policies but as a European Left governing paradigm within a hostile domestic and international environment. Moreover, many believed that Greece was the latest and probably the most important battleground in the financial sector's elite war on democracy (Monbiot 2015).

SYRIZA came to power declaring that the Troika was "history" and promising, among other things, according to Antoniou (2016), to do the following:

- End austerity and renegotiate the country's bailout with the Troika
- Write off most of the foreign debt while repaying the remainder in line with Greece's economic growth
- Halt privatizations and abolish the property tax
- Increase the minimum monthly wage
- Increase public allowances for those below the poverty line
- Reinstate the Christmas bonus pension
- Provide free medical care for the unemployed
- Oppose repossession of people's homes

The basis and rationale for this agenda of radical reform were outlined in the "Thessaloniki Manifesto" (SYRIZA 2014), which focused on the country's severe humanitarian crisis.

Nevertheless, as soon as the party was elected, SYRIZA abandoned any talk of fundamental changes (Petras 2015b). First, the party accepted the legitimacy of the country's overall foreign debt, which in the past it had questioned. At his inauguration ceremony Tsipras (2015) stated his intention to negotiate for a mutually fair solution and Finance Minister, Y. Varoufakis, asked for a "transitional bridge agreement" in order to buy time (Agourides 2015). Moreover, although it had promised to cancel the Memorandum if elected, SYRIZA did no such thing.

Second, and related to the preceding, SYRIZA declared its determination to remain in the EU and the Eurozone, hinting at a limited ability to fashion an independent policy. Furthermore, in an effort to alleviate any fears, Tsipras (2015) declared that his government "had no intention of threatening the balance of power within the EU". Third, SYRIZA did not question Greece's support of the NATO military policies. Fourth, a significant number of Tsipras cabinet appointees were from academia with no experience with real politics; and, even more surprising, some were former PASOK advisers and members with no power or willingness to break with the dictates of the Troika (Spourdalakis 2016).

While the Greek government played for time (Agourides 2015), creditors pushed for compliance with their terms. Amid speculation of a possible *Grexit*, on 11 February 2015 the Greek government submitted a request for a six-month extension for its loan repayment; the creditors agreed to four months. The agreement initiated a period of constructive ambiguity wherein the creditors issued warnings over the state of Greece's economy.

Some analysts saw this as a sign of either naivety or retreat (e.g., Spourdalakis 2015; Seferiades 2015); for others it was a sign of SYRIZA's decision to remain in power at any cost (Mpogiopoulos 2015). Whatever the case, under pressure from the Troika and other European governments, the party began to move away from its earlier promises—in much the same way as PASOK had done earlier—and followed a linear course towards softening its programmatic policies.

The party position regarding the foreign debt was most telling of this turnaround (Mavroudeas 2015). At first, it declared that it would not accept the country's foreign debt in its entirety and that if elected it would be written off. As the chance of governing became more realistic, the party changed its position, calling for the unilateral cancelling of *part* of the debt; it then changed position again, this time to the "consensual" deletion of part of the debt. Following its election to office, SYRIZA adopted a new approach, calling for the repayment period to be extended in relation to the growth of the economy.

As it gradually yielded to the Troika demands, the government turned to a strategy of communications management and symbolic actions (Anastasiou 2015). In this regard we note that the Troika was renamed the "institutions," and that the Troika technocrats no longer worked in the ministries but in their hotel rooms. The government also tried to shift the agenda to more favourable issues, focusing on the need to address the humanitarian crisis caused by previous Memorandums. It was during this period that the government (unsuccessfully) sought finances from Russia, China, and Latin America (Antoniou 2016). The fact that they seriously thought that, most notably, Russia would be able and willing to bankroll a

Grexit, as it was struggling through an economic crisis of its own as well as EU and US sanctions, is painful proof of its lack of understanding of the international political context (Mudde 2015: 82).

SYRIZA's February compromise and the gradual convergence of its program with the Memorandum led to the first test of its coherence as a governing party. Its inherent centrifugal tendencies once again unravelled, signalling a period of intraparty crisis. Initially, the communist faction of SYRIZA called for an extraordinary conference to elect a new party leadership, while also asking the MPs not to vote for the agreement.[2] A long-standing and much respected party member, EMP M. Glezos (2015), publicly apologized to the people of Greece because he had colluded in the new government's deception.

After months of fruitless negotiations, which actually worsened the country's bargaining power, the international creditors offered a bailout plan to the Greek government (3 June). This was rejected, and a counterproposal was presented,[3] which the creditors did not accept. In these proposals, however, there was little of the "radical left" regarding the softening of austerity (Mudde 2015: 79). On 26 June, Tsipras took everyone by surprise when he called for a referendum on the proposals of Commission President Mr. Junker. On 28 June the banks closed down and capital controls were imposed. The referendum vote took place on 5 July 2015 and the Greek electorate by a large majority (61.31 %) rejected the Junker proposals amid intense polarization (Sygkelos 2015).

Armed with the popular "no," Tsipras travelled to Brussels to negotiate a better deal. However, he came back from Brussels, having accepted a third and even harsher Memorandum, claiming he had no alternative because the Greeks were attached to the euro (Petras 2015b). As Tsipras framed it, the choice was between the bailout (which SYRIZA ultimately signed) and a series of even worse policies that would have been agreed to by the parties of the centre-right and Right. In July the government submitted a list of policy commitments and actions to be taken in consultation with the EC/ECB/IMF, signalling that it had accepted the majority of the Troika demands including: privatizations, abolishment of various subsidies, reforms (i.e., decreases) to the pension system, and outside review and evaluation of the whole range of existing labour market arrangements taking into account best practices elsewhere in Europe (i.e., flexicurity), among others.

That new Memorandum (13 July) contained a host of neo-liberal measures that represented an ideological setback for SYRIZA and was harshly received. Some called this transformation a process "from the absurd to the tragic" (Kouvelakis 2015); others said that it was "a total reversal of the popular verdict through condensed and highly opaque procedures" (Seferiades 2015). Petras (2015c) called it an "electoral fraud." From a broader European perspective, the Greek referendum was a symbolic victory. "But such victories are exactly that, symbolic, and tend to not last long" (Mudde 2015: 64). Tsipras's main aim was to increase his power within his own party; this he would accomplish, he felt, by weeding out the (real) radicals, and thus taking full control with his own people (ibid., p. 101).

Spourdalakis (2015, 2016) framed it as "a big fall-back, a big defeat" that should be understood however as a turning point in a long war waged by the Left for control of state power. In his words, "it was a manoeuvre in front of incredibly more powerful forces, an EU coup in order to save strength and maintain the ability to continue the war in the future."[4] Whatever the case and whatever the reason, it concluded a period of rapid de-radicalization of party positions with SYRIZA taking a crucial blow both programmatically and morally (Moschonas 2015b: 26).

Tsipras about-turn is a clear example of how the experience gained in office can fundamentally change the way leaders make arguments; although Tsipras claimed that the bailout deal he struck was the very best that was on offer, he had earlier called a very similar scenario a plan to "humiliate" Greece (Hough and Olsen 2015). Yet there were many who believed that SYRIZA's handling of the situation reflected ideological naivety, amateurism, and unintelligent leadership (Seferiades 2015; Mudde 2015: 80). This attitude can perhaps be understood in the context of the party's sudden success in Greece, which several leading party figures felt could be reproduced just as easily in a European context (Spourdalakis 2016).

SYRIZA hoped to promote its policies simply by appealing to the loftier values of Europe and pleading for kinder treatment. Moreover, Tsipras and SYRIZA assured everyone that there could be no question of abandoning the euro, thus rendering their threats for a possible Grexit less credible. "The EU elite were confronted with a petitioner without a card in its hand and had no reason to make any concessions" (Lapavitsas 2016; Anderson 2015). Moreover, as Mudde (2015: 55–60) suggested, by accepting the bailout the party strengthened the belief among opponents that (all) Eurosceptics were necessarily incompetent and moralistic.

The government therefore pursued negotiations within the confines of a soft neo-liberalism (Anastasiou 2015)—a form of controlled austerity for the lower social strata without inciting a direct conflict with established power structures and practices. This was justified using the pretext of dealing with the humanitarian crisis. The party's narrative resembled the Italian Communist Party (PCI) rhetoric of the 1970s (see Chap. 1); it was not the time for a total rupture. It was felt that the government should aim to restore the country's prospects for development and the normality of the precrisis era.

On 14 August the agreement was approved by the Greek parliament; the SYRIZA government passed the bill only because the opposition parties supported it; that is, 39 SYRIZA parliamentarians either abstained or voted against it (Agourides 2015). The one-time anti-austerity champions of SYRIZA and ANEL signed the new austerity deal and the third Memorandum was now a reality. The signing of it tested the party's unity once again. For example, the SYRIZA Youth (2015) demanded Tsipras's resignation; R. Rinaldi (2015), leader of the Maoist Greek Communist Organization (KOE), resigned on 21 July 2015, with another 17 members of SYRIZA's Central Committee following suit a few days later.[5] The crest of these reactions was the creation of a new party by SYRIZA dissidents—the Popular Unity (LAE) on 21 August 2015—led by P. Lafazanis.[6] Because of the intense reactions within SYRIZA, on 20 August, Tsipras announced that the popular mandate had "worn out" and called for new elections.

CHANGING THE NARRATIVE ONCE AGAIN: THE PARALLEL PROGRAMME

SYRIZA had won the January elections by promising a very specific programme (the Thessaloniki Programme); forced to back down, the party simultaneously called for new elections and proposed a new strategy called the "parallel programme" (SYRIZA 2015: 21). It exclusively emphasized internal issues such as fighting corruption, upgrading local government, democratizing public administration, ending tax evasion, and so on—all of which were thought to undermine the reproductive core of Greek capitalism. SYRIZA denounced criticism that it endorsed neo-liberalism, explaining its acceptance of the third Memorandum as a temporary and tactical compromise (SYRIZA 2015: 6). Tsipras declared on many occasions that the party was forced to accept a Memorandum in which it did not believe as a tactical manoeuvre, indirectly referring to Lenin's well-known "two steps back, one step forward."

Recognizing that any substantive changes to the Memorandum were impossible at the national level, the SYRIZA government tried to compensate by politicizing the issue on the supranational (EU) level. Using this strategy, the party stressed that the forces of resistance can make cracks in the almighty neo-liberal paradigm. According to this narrative, when new developments arise (i.e., when other leftist parties, such as Podemos, achieve government), they will be able to more easily advocate for radical change.

Elections were held on 20 September 2015, and it was clear that Tsipras was using them to reinforce his position within and beyond his own party, with some believing that his call for rapid elections was designed to secure votes from a shocked electorate before the pain of his transformation had been fully felt (Petras 2015c). Nevertheless, SYRIZA's about-turn did not, in spite of what most opinion polls predicted, cause any great damage to the party. As the September election illustrated, although the 25 SYRIZA parliamentarians who left to form their own political party (LAE) may have had ideological purity on their side, they did not have the Greek people with them. Most Greeks were tired of fighting with the rest of Europe and were anxious to move forward; SYRIZA's deal was seen as helping it do that and thus the party kept its popular appeal. There, however, were certain other factors that helped SYRIZA maintain its popularity including: being new, presenting itself as a "fighter" against Europe, and remaining pro-European (Kiapidou 2015b).

By the end of 2015 the party had abandoned its parallel programme (*Kathimerini*, 18 December 2015). Following severe objections from the Euro Working Group, the SYRIZA government had to withdraw even the draft legislation presented in parliament that included measures to implement its programme. Symbolically, at least, this development was a serious defeat for the leftist government, which insisted that despite its many concessions to creditors the parallel programme would bring some relief to those who most needed it. Unable to deal with their European counterparts, the government chose to focus on internal corruption and tax evasion (*Avgi*, 27 December 2015, p. 2).

The Party–Government Relationship

Although the party–government relationship often is based on oversimplification (Cotta 1999), it remains crucial to the smooth running of the government, the optimal electoral performance of the party, and the preservation of party identity. This last factor is particularly important for RLPs that want to emphasize their distinctiveness. In the case of SYRIZA, although the party–government relationship was extensively analyzed by party academics and the party-affiliated research institute of N. Poulantzas before the party achieved governing power (Spourdalakis 2015), it proved to be a totally different case once the party took office. This once again proved that reality is significantly different from theoretical analyses.

The party's major challenge was to continue and even advance the strategy that had brought it to power by enhancing its presence in the social field and avoiding cartelization (Spourdalakis 2014: 363). SYRIZA saw this as critical for maintaining the party's radical orientation, as was the democratization of public institutions. In this regard, the party needed to not only justify and support the democratic reforms of the government but also had to find ways to push it further in favour of the class interests that it represented.

Vernardakis (2015), party member, academic, and government minister, warned early on that to place government over party would be a strategic and historic mistake since it would undermine the party's ability to maintain its distinct identity and communicate and represent society. In practice though, appointing party cadres to government positions not only weakened party organization but also contributed to cartelization of it. Thus, SYRIZA reproduced post-democratic trends whereby the party in government sidelines other components of the party (Papadopoulou and Spourdalakis 2015).

Another issue that put the party's moral advantage in jeopardy was its involvement in the clientelistic practices of the past, whereby relatives and close friends of governing and party officials are appointed to posts in the government apparatus. Moreover, the party's traditional educational function was abandoned; that is, there was no longer any theoretical or education work to ensure the consolidation of "the SYRIZA way," while new members—a number that quadrupled—were not given time to become socialized within the party's radical culture (Spourdalakis 2016).

The sudden growth of the party facilitated de-radicalization. In the 2012 elections SYRIZA's parliamentary representation grew to 79 MPs compared to only 14 in 2009; after the January 2015 elections the number increased to 149 (two short of a parliamentary majority). The increased representation of the party in public office had several important implications. First, the focus of the party's strategy changed from the street to parliament, emphasizing elections and parliamentary coalitions with traditional parties (Spourdalakis 2015). Second, SYRIZA's electoral success in 2012 served as a substitute for social mobilization, and, in that sense, the party prioritized its quick advancement to power, hoping to be able to cancel austerity policies.

Third, the parliamentary team superseded party organs; this became very clear when the 15 July 2015 agreement was discussed with the parliamentary group before being discussed with the party's central committee. At the same time, the party bureaucracy functioned as a shadow government, eventually leading to the weakening of the party's collective bodies. Strategic decisions were made by only a few government officials without consultation with party organs. All organizational and ideological processes that would lead to further development were paused as the rise in government accelerated.

Because of its stunted organizational development, the central party and the leadership became even more important (Eleftheriou 2015: 71). Moreover, following his win in the 2015 elections, Tsipras systematically promoted the image of a "responsible" prime minister who was not under party control but functioned as a "representative of the nation" as a whole. As a result, Tsipras has enjoyed much wider public acceptance than his party. A personalization (i.e., presidentialization) of party politics was largely at work in this regard. All the preceding led to signs of autonomous activity at all levels, especially at the top, which undermined the party's cohesion and its links to a number of social movements. All these, taken together, indicate an alienation of the SYRIZA leadership from the party's radical physiognomy (Spourdalakis 2016).

Beyond Keynes

It was evident from the outset that the SYRIZA government would have trouble defending its left-wing ideology against the EU's institutional and political "conservatism." In opposing EU policies, SYRIZA was sure to test not only the limits of the EU but also the limits of its own identity. Understanding this, even before the elections SYRIZA started to compromise on its more radical positions. When it first entered the Greek political scene as a contender in 2012, it did so on a radical Left platform that bore all the features of a party in opposition. Emphasizing anti-establishment ideas, SYRIZA declared that it would renegotiate austerity at any cost. As the party got closer to power, however, it started to resemble a party in office; it began to moderate its position in a bid to attract broader electoral support.

SYRIZA's "moral crusade" against capitalism ended when it accepted the Memorandum. All aspects of the party's electoral programme were sidelined either explicitly or implicitly (Sevastakis 2015: 28). Contrary to its promises, the party failed to: (1) restore pension payments; (2) restore the minimum wage; (3) reverse privatizations; (4) end austerity programmes; and (5) increase funds for education, health, housing, and local development. Moreover, the Defence Minister offered new military bases for NATO, including an air–naval base on the Greek island of Karpathos. SYRIZA hid its inability, or reluctance, to implement its programme with symbolic moves and by prioritizing the Troika negotiations. This inconsistency led to confusion among the public and resulted in the party being branded as unreliable.

Although predicting the future is best left to the oracles, SYRIZA is likely to move in a more mainstream direction, making tough decisions and then struggling with the consequences; the party is not likely to return to its original programme. "Tsipras might have threatened to press the self-destruct button on a number of occasions, but ultimately the attractions of power and the sheer doggedness of a party determined to defend itself and survive won out" (Hough and Olsen 2015). Despite its vocal opposition, SYRIZA in fact implemented a neo-liberal austerity policy, which not only contradicts its ideological profile and preelectoral pledges but also refuted the party's entire history and past political practice. SYRIZA has essentially accepted the dilemma that plagued the mainstream political parties—that is, Memorandum or default. The party tended to blame all its, and the country's, misfortunes on external inevitabilities and on the "reactionary forces of Europe" (Tsipras 2016; Dragasakis 2016), while party failures were seen as the fault of certain individuals (Sevastakis 2015: 29).

There are very obvious similarities between SYRIZA after the 2015 elections and PASOK in 1974–1981. For example, the term "socialism" had been expunged from both parties' vocabulary (although occasionally used by the SYRIZA leadership with internal audiences), and SYRIZA's rhetoric on anti-austerity benefited the party much like PASOK's call in the 1970s for exiting NATO and the European Economic Community (EEC) benefited it. The party's radicalism subsided very quickly after its January 2015 election victory, just as PASOK toned down its socialist ideology during its time in government. Mudde (2015: 35) believed that SYRIZA would play roughly the same role in the Greek party system that PASOK had for decades (i.e., provide the populist left-wing alternative to the conservative ND).

AKEL AT THE CROSSROADS

The Cypriot Left presidency also can be divided into two distinct periods. The first period covers the years 2008–2011 when the emphasis was on negotiations for a solution to the Cyprus Problem, and the second period covers the years 2011–2013 when the economy took precedence. When Christofias and AKEL took over in early 2008, the economy was doing well, and with the CTP still in power in the north, there seemed to be a historic opportunity for the Left to solve the Cyprus Problem. In the early stages, the right-wing DISY refrained from criticizing the new government, giving it time and space to proceed with the negotiations, while the centrist parties—the Movement for Social Democracy, EDEK, and the Democratic Party of Cyprus, DIKO, known as hardliners on the problem—were then partners in the government. At the international and European levels reactions to Christofias's election were mostly positive.

Gradually though, as progress in the negotiations stalled, and as the economic situation began to deteriorate (in early 2010), criticism against the government became more vocal and political attacks against it became more aggressive. EDEK exited the government coalition in February 2010, alleging that Christofias had made unacceptable concessions in the negotiations with the Turkish side; and by 2011 the AKEL government was operating in a very hostile environment. Christofias himself had become the main target of a sustained offensive not only by the Right and the Church leadership, but also by a variety of social and political actors, opinion leaders, and the media. Christofias's poor statesmanship also alienated many of the liberal, social-democratic Left, as well as those voters for whom management skills, personality, and communication strategy were important (Charalambous and Ioannou 2015: 9).

Christofias's economic policies in the early stages of his administration were mildly Keynesian: public spending increased and the privatization of state-run enterprises was categorically ruled out. This was not a revolutionary practice; it was rather an old (Left) social democratic policy no longer commonly found in EU member states. The AKEL-led government strengthened the welfare state by increasing provisions for allowances and benefits by 42 % (*Simerini*, 27 November 2011) and by boosting the minimum wage per month from 699 to 855 euros, as well as introducing a scheme for increasing low-level pensions and launching a comprehensive low-income housing policy. In addition, it attempted twice, unsuccessfully, to impose taxation on profits and large land ownership.

Other than that, however, both at home and in the European domain, the party was reluctant to introduce radical proposals (Katsourides 2012). For example, in an obvious attempt to calm the "markets," the first Finance Minister (as well as his two successors) was a high-ranking executive at Cyprus's largest bank, which some interpreted as indicative of ties to capitalism that would infringe on the party's political and organizational autonomy (Charalambous and Ioannou 2015: 11).

Party euphoria at its rise to power was reflected in the 2010 Congress. Christofias's election was considered the most momentous landmark in the party's history, and a chance for the working class to finally prosper (AKEL 2010b: 2–3). Although AKEL still considered the EU an advanced form of capitalist integration with an anti-labour orientation and anti-democratic structures, it also thought that it could be an arena for claiming the workers and the people's rights (AKEL 2010b: 7–10). The party criticized the neo-liberal EU policies, claiming that they increasingly and negatively affected Cypriots lives—a stance that seems to reflect a partial reideologization of the EU issue as well as a way to deflect criticism from the party's deficiencies and lack of radicalization (by transferring the responsibility to the EU bodies).

By and large no one understood the potential threat to Cyprus of the economic crisis. Therefore, at the first signs of the crisis the party had to respond both theoretically and in practice. A Marxist framework was used to analyze the causes of the crisis (AKEL 2010b: 3), while proposals for its solution fell within a Keynesian frame. AKEL viewed the crisis mainly as a failure of the neo-liberal version of capitalism, and it sought solutions that would mitigate the effects of the crisis on workers, foster growth, and ensure market accountability.

As the economic crisis began to materialize, the government introduced several austerity measures. The 2011 measures were not extremely harsh on the working class and the popular strata in general, compared to those adopted in 2012 and that are still in effect.[7] Nevertheless, the economic reforms proposed in November 2011 revealed underlying party tensions. Some of these proposed measures included a 2 % increase in the VAT—an indirect form of taxation that the party had traditionally opposed—and a two-year freeze on wage increases. AKEL initially rejected the proposals and emphasized wealth taxation instead (*Haravgi*, 20 November 2011); a few days later, however, emphasizing that this compromise contradicted the party's position, it conceded (Secretary General A. Kyprianou in *Kathimerini*, 19 February 2012).

In 2011 the full force of the economic crisis began to be felt. At the same time the government was found responsible for a July 2011 deadly explosion at a naval base. Now AKEL's last remaining coalition partner, DIKO, departed and the government was under enormous pressure to adopt austerity measures and privatization (Fischer and Economou 2015; Panayiotou 2014: 42). Christofias originally responded with pleas to preserve the "tripartite understanding" between the state, labour unions, and business interests; at the same time, he tried to buy time by successfully applying to Russia for a loan (€5bn) hoping that the crisis would subside and a European solution would be found. A similar attempt to get a loan from China did not bear fruit.

When the Russian money began to run out and it refused to give an additional loan, the president decided he had nothing left to lose. He pointed to the capitalist origins of the crisis, denounced the markets as "thieves of the globe," and blamed the banks for the collapse of the Cypriot economy. At the same time, and unable to implement the more radical aspects of its programme, the government and the party launched a joint public campaign trying to convey the message that not only they implemented a host of measures but also that these measures were in fact to the benefit of the poplar strata (e.g., see AKEL 2011b). This campaign was aimed mostly at the traditional leftist constituency that the party feared it was alienating. But this radical turn came too late; it had no impact on the government or AKEL's electoral fortunes, and it was undermined by a government decision to apply to the Troika for financial help in the summer of 2012.

Although both the opposition and the media put enormous pressure on the president to apply for monetary help, threatening that failure to do so would even inflict criminal responsibilities,[8] AKEL was placed in a very difficult position. The measures demanded by the lenders violated fundamental party positions (e.g., privatizations, social cuts, changes in the automatic price indexing). Even though the government condemned the Troika stance and did not officially sign an agreement, in the absence of any alternative, it was forced to submit. The party voted for the parliamentary bills that brought this agreement into effect (House of Representatives 2012). AKEL seemed ready to take the path of the post-1990s international social democracy, effectively adopting a neo-liberal logic because, as it said, "there was simply no other alternative" (Charalambous and Ioannou 2015: 11).

Notwithstanding the generalized neo-liberal offensive against AKEL, the Christofias tenure seemed to have reinforced a view held by some of the Cypriot Left that AKEL was little more than yet another social democratic enterprise (Fischer and Economou 2015). Although AKEL should not be considered a revolutionary party, the notion that it shared the neo-liberal outlook of the Greek PASOK or the British Labour Party is, to say the least, wrongheaded. AKEL is a Left reformist party with a character that is informed by class as well as the specific circumstances in which it operate.

Christofias was elected under the slogan, "For a just solution to the Cyprus problem and a just society" (Christophorou 2008). Regardless of his responsibilities amid the huge economic crisis, his presidency was perceived as traitorous to his promises. By the time of the next presidential elections in 2013, the credibility of the party and the government was so tarnished that for the first time AKEL faced considerable obstacles while trying to rally its supporters around its chosen candidate; 25 % of its constituency voted contrary to party choice in the presidential election of February 2013. Moreover, it was left without allies. It was clear that AKEL's tenure of executive power had proved very costly to the party; the government, the party, and especially the president experienced extreme public disapproval. Additionally, during Christofias's five-year tenure, the party and the Left trade union (PEO) were tied up in defusing the members and the voters grievances, emphasizing parliamentary solutions and social dialogue.

The 2014 European elections and the 2016 national elections verified the downward electoral turn. In 2014 the party scored 26.98 %, losing almost 8 % compared to the 2009 European elections (34.9 %). AKEL polled merely 25.67 % in the 2016 national elections, down by 7 % from 2011—an electoral low in the party's history. AKEL also suffered a huge decline in actual numbers: in a period of five years the party lost approximately 42,000 voters. Although many reasons can be cited to explain this decline, most analyses seem to agree that the main reason was the consequence of the party's hold of the executive.

In retrospect, Christofias's presidency can be judged in two opposing ways: as an attempt to withstand the pressures of neo-liberalization on the one hand and as a de-radicalization of party positions on the other. The party managed to introduce only small changes to the system (e.g., some subsidies and welfare services were initially increased and later saved from more drastic cuts); this was termed as a strategy of delaying and avoiding direct confrontation until the time was suitable. Although this should not be underestimated, no one could argue that socialism was around the corner. Moreover, not even one of the government electoral programme's more radical proposals (e.g., educational reform and reduction of the term of compulsory military service) was realized.

In explaining these failures, the argument has been made that AKEL was not prepared for governing (Panayiotou 2014: 54) for two main reasons. First, because the party (wrongly) believed that it was accepted as a legitimate actor, it was slow to respond effectively to political and social attacks; second, the party had lost its ability to mobilize after ten years in office (2003–2013). Nevertheless, AKEL did bring forward issues that had been taboo for many decades (e.g., Greek Cypriot responsibilities for the Cyprus Problem). Moreover, the Left presidency inherited the task of finalizing the research and drilling licences for the natural gas in Cyprus's Exclusive Economic Zone, which it successfully carried out (Panayiotou 2014: 19). Despite this success, for a first time in its history and only a few years after taking office, AKEL was regarded as a mainstream party, no different from the rest of the office-seeking political elite. No longer could the party claim convincingly that it represented the common people, and no longer did the common people see AKEL as their genuine defender against daily injustices (Charalambous and Ioannou 2015: 3).

The Party–Government Nexus

The party–government relationship was a key issue, and from the very beginning the party declared that it should maintain its distinctiveness from the government although supporting it (AKEL 2008). On examination it appears that the party differentiated itself from the government only twice: first, when it voted against the Treaty of Lisbon (July 2008), and second, when it voted down the new European Commission (February 2010). On both occasions, it was known in advance that the party's negative vote would not affect the (positive) outcome.

As noted earlier (see Chap. 4), AKEL never engaged in a genuine ideological discussion either internally or with other Leftist elements in Cyprus. This has been evident in its lack of theoretical analyses on such an important and controversial issue as the governing-party relationship. The party's policy proposals and its (very few) ideological analyses were always left to the central leadership; as a result, during AKEL's tenure in government, policy-making reflected the government's political and electoral interests (Charalambous and Ioannou 2015: 12).

AKEL's involvement with various segments of the electorate, which strongly opposed the austerity measures taken by the Christofias administration, led to expectations of behavioural pluralism, at least at the parliamentary level. The institutional structure of the Cyprus Republic has been conducive to such behaviour because, although the executive did not rest on parliamentary majority, by the same token the party was free from obligations of strict loyalty. However, this never happened.

Parliamentarians and key party officials, some of whom were also government officials, were ubiquitous in AKEL's decision-making settings, ensuring that the party in government maintained control over the whole of its organization. Neither the trade unions nor the rest of the party's ancillary or affiliated organizations ever questioned the linkage between party and government. The organic element in AKEL's relationship with the Popular Movement tampered with, rather than reinforced, the latter's influence on the government. Neither the party press, *Haravgi*, nor any of the party's published materials and leadership rhetoric made any attempt to promote anything other than support of the government.

AKEL was identified completely with the government and the president himself, and therefore, any faults stemming from the executive cast a negative light on the party. The fact that the president was able to pursue policies seemingly at odds with AKEL's official policies was mostly because of two reasons: (1) Christofias's strong hold over the party leadership built throughout his 21-year tenure as General Secretary and (2) the party's fear that criticism of the government would only facilitate the opposition's strategy to de-legitimize it.

With the end of Christofias's tenure in government in February 2013, AKEL immediately became radicalized again, thus highlighting the impact of government-opposition dynamics. No longer tied to government, suffering significant electoral losses, and fearing further partisan detachment, AKEL declared itself ready to fight against the Troika and the Cypriot government's neo-liberal policies (AKEL 2014: 5). It proposed Cyprus's exit from the Eurozone as the only way out of the bail-in that the new right-wing government had agreed to with the Troika (AKEL 2013), and the party led the way in demonstrations and legislative bills against the Memorandum measures. In addition, it submitted a bill asking for the postponement of privatizations until the end of 2017,[9] it declared its intention to renationalize those public companies that would be privatized,[10] and the PEO led the way to restoring past workers' achievements (Kyritsis 2015). Nonetheless, the party's time in government had negatively affected its ability and/or willingness to mobilize protest. Moreover, the party's efforts at re-ideologization were seen by many as largely hypocritical.

To absorb post-election tensions within the party, AKEL initiated an internal assessment process that culminated in a programmatic congress early in 2014. AKEL was eager to end all internal discussion and criticism of its government performance prior to the electoral congress of 2015 and the parliamentary elections of May 2016. The party analysis presented at the programmatic congress (AKEL 2014) made it clear that AKEL wanted to blame its failures on the EU, the banks, and the opposition parties. The party also declared its determination to fight austerity and to find ways to exit from the Memorandum measures; however, it had no concrete solutions, only vague references to growth stimulation and the need to maintain public ownership of state-owned enterprises.

No matter how unpleasant the Christofias government may have been for party supporters, the leadership almost totally avoided any kind of self-criticism (Charalambous and Ioannou 2015: 13). Social bipolarism always has been so resilient within AKEL's ranks that self-criticism and even genuine soul-searching always have been seen, especially now, as conceding ground to the Right, thus undermining the Left's competitive position within the party system. The party has never tolerated any manifestation of disagreement, believing that self-critical behaviour would only serve to empower the Right and thus, indirectly but inevitably, harm the working class.

In retrospect, this also explains, at least in part, why a heterogeneous support base translated into a homogeneous internal culture that never seriously challenged the leadership. Within AKEL there was a great tendency to accept the opinions and/or interpretations of the leadership on all major and complex questions (e.g., EU participation, power hold, and political strategy). The idea that only the current leadership represented "true" leftist politics and that those who disagreed with any of its positions represented "leftism" or opportunism had been well established. Moreover, the lack of any type of internal or external outlet for channelling dissent led most dissenters to completely withdraw from politics. There might be another reason, though: party activists and members may have preferred to avoid any soul-searching or questioning of the belief system they grew up with.

Despite the problems that government participation caused the party, AKEL over and over reiterated its belief that any communist party was "obliged to pursue government participation even within capitalism as a means to materialize its policies" (e.g., see AKEL 2014: 36).

It acknowledged that this should be done with a radical programme, but radicalism had to be defined according to the specific circumstances in a specific country at a specific time. In this respect, the meaning of radicalism differs from time to time, from place to place. Once again, therefore, it is clear that claiming power must be analyzed through the prism of each country's particularities, which, in Cyprus's case, required AKEL to claim power by finding a solution to the Cyprus Problem.

Caught Between Continuity (Past) and Transformation (Future)

Christofias's election served both to unlock the Cypriot party system and to highlight the challenges of AKEL's radical identity. The difficult choice between the "vote-policy-office" trichotomy of party goals was at the heart of this problem. Reluctance to radicalize once in office can be explained by a number of factors. First, at the core of AKEL politics was the perception that the social, political, and international contexts within which party politics unfold inhibits fundamental changes to the existing social system (Katsourides 2012: 202). Cyprus's small size, its dependency on the EU, and its lack of global influence were indicative of the international limitations placed on the party, and underlined AKEL's inability to alter the systemic variables of the capitalist system on its own. At the same time, however, this belief was at odds with the party's justification—that is, changing the system from within—for altering its position on the EU issue, as well as for taking over government portfolios.

Although the party did not change its stance on the EU during the Christofias administration, there was clearly tension between the party rhetoric and government practice (Charalambous 2012b). The party strategy regarding the EU was focused primarily on taking positions that were viable in the short run and also different from those of the Right; to a lesser extent, it targeted any type of rupture with existing economic and social relations. Especially while in government, the party disavowed its theoretical programme and silently accepted EU policies and directives. In this regard, AKEL's stance towards the EU combined mild ideological criticism and pragmatism, the latter being the most obvious. AKEL's lack of a rigorous Left Europeanism reflected both the party's belief that Cyprus was too small to affect EU decision-making mechanisms, and its fear of being domestically accused as anti-European in a country that largely remained pro-EU. This also could explain and be related to the party-led government's lack of resistance to neo-liberal policies while in office despite some exaggerated rhetoric.

Domestically, it was the unresolved Cyprus Problem that guided AKEL's policies and forced it to restrain from presenting an agenda that was too socialist. Without the "excuse" of solving the Cyprus Problem, AKEL would have been ideologically bound to promote a socialist project, and the party understood that this most certainly would lead to their marginalization and or rejection. With this line of argument, therefore, the party was seen as very politically shrewd to use the Cyprus Problem as a way to avoid "Left criticism" of its policies. The party itself argued that it followed a course consistent with its communist heritage and ideology (Stephanou interview, cited in Katsourides 2012). It contended that Cyprus's most pressing duty was to ensure the country's independence and to solve the Cyprus Problem, so the party sidelined its ideological projects.

Cyprus's political system raised further obstacles for radical programmes and substantive institutional changes. Political alliances were imperative because one party could not command a majority, and this directly affected the political programme adopted by any candidate. Christofias's manifesto for the presidency reflected this and was constructed to accommodate the divergent views of possible allies (e.g., political parties), avoid controversial issues (e.g., taxing the Church's business activities), and secure backing of powerful domestic actors (e.g., trade unions of government employees, banks, etc.). As a result, the party was required to play down its working-class discourse and to develop stances that would be acceptable to supporters of capitalism and a free market. That limited its capacity to develop and to implement authentic radical policies when in office.

AKEL has been reformist, pragmatic, and "constructively shy" in its demands since its very inception (Charalambous and Ioannou 2015: 15). While not in government, this strategy worked well both electorally and in building up a Left counterculture to the dominant discourse of nationalism, conservatism, and neo-liberalism. Despite its history of consensus-seeking, AKEL remained an alternative party with a perceived theoretical radicalism that potentially could materialize somehow. Nevertheless, once AKEL took executive office its opponents became exponentially more aggressive, such that this reformism no longer worked.

The party choice to uphold its long-standing strategy while simultaneously sublimating its more radical objectives to strictly electoral objectives proved ineffective. It did not prevent the Right from achieving a sweeping victory in subsequent elections, nor did it address or honour working-class interests. The Left, however, contributed to the demystification and deconstruction of various aspects of the hegemonic context within which the Cyprus Problem historically was perceived, as well as proposed solutions to the economic crisis that would place a greater burden on the privileged societal strata.

Now, three years after leaving government, AKEL seems yet unable to recover although it attempted to play a key role in recent anti-Troika and anti-government mobilizations. The party is faced with problems affecting all established parties in the era of "post-democracy" (Crouch 2004). Because of its earlier experience in government, it fails to be widely perceived as an "anti-establishment" party, and this is reinforced by the lack of any real social struggle in contemporary Cyprus (Katsourides 2016, forthcoming). The discredit of the party, together with the ongoing process of de-alignment, has created a niche to the left of the party.

Despite indications of the party's de-radicalization, important elements of its radical identity have been retained. For example, the party remains in favour of an alternative social arrangement, progressive taxation, social provision, and allowances for the poorer strata of society (AKEL 2010b, 2014, 2015b). However, the radical aspects of the party's overall policies and positions have been downgraded in its public agenda, and they are secondary to the aims of electoral politics. The party realizes that the only feasible target in the era of the so-called "New Order" is to preserve and, if possible, enhance the traditional social democratic welfare consensus rather than agitating for a total transformation of society. In this regard, government participation represents the best way to weaken the power and influence of the Right.

Overall, the party's course in government reflects both a process of de-radicalization, on the one hand, and AKEL's lack of readiness to cope with the requirements of governing, on the other. The party doctrines reflect what has been identified as the typical RLPs' defence strategy; because the parties are unable or unwilling to implement key policies, they aim instead to prevent a more pronounced drift towards neo-liberalism (Bale and Dunphy 2011).

Notes

1. http://www.telegraph.co.uk/news/worldnews/europe/greece/11421671/Veteran-conservative-Prokopis-Pavlopoulos-elected-Greek-president.html; accessed 22 February 2015.
2. http://www.marxismos.com/greece-menu/24-greek-politics/syn-syriza/2315-sumfonia-upotagis.html; accessed 22 February 2015.
3. http://blogs.ft.com/brusselsblog/2015/06/05/leaked-greeces-new-debt-restructuring-plan/, 5 June 2015; accessed 22 September 2015.

4. The party perception that the financial institutions actually carried out an economic coup against SYRIZA to avoid a further leftist turn in other European countries was enhanced when WikiLeaks released a transcription of teleconferencing conversations between IMF officials threatening Greece with a "credit event" before the Grexit referendum. See, http://big.assets.huffingtonpost.com/IMFF.pdf; accessed 4 April 2016.
5. Statement of Resignation, http://www.e-dromos.gr/dilosi-18/; accessed 31 July 2015.
6. Popular Unity: 25 SYRIZA MPs Form a New Parliamentary Team, http://iskra.gr/index.php?option=com_content&view=article&id=21783:laikh-enothta&catid=83:aristera&Itemid=200; accessed 21 August 2015.
7. Overall, 65 legislative bills were introduced from 26 August 2011 until 17 January 2013 by the Christofias administration in order to address the economic downfall and to comply with the Troika demands. These bills included, among others, measures for limiting public spending, cuts in welfare allowances and salaries, and further liberalizing sectors of the economy. See Committee of Finance, House of Representatives, Memorandum-related legislation, internal document, undated.
8. See President N. Anastasiades's open letter to Christofias, 16 November 2012, http://www.sigmalive.com/news/politics/22151/parousiazoume-tin-epistoli-anastasiadi-ston-xristofia; accessed 12 January 2016.
9. http://www.philenews.com/el-gr/oikonomia-kypros/146/281540/protasi-nomou-kata-ton-idiotikopoiiseon, 15 October 2015; accessed 22 January 2016.
10. http://www.sigmalive.com/news/politics/291654/metopo-kata-apokratikopoiisis-tis-cyta-apo-antipolitefsi, 12 December 2015; accessed 22 December 2015.

BIBLIOGRAPHY

Agourides, Y. (2015). 'Battles, Victories, Defeats, Compromises and new Negotiations', *Avgi* 27 December, pp. 4–5.
AKEL (2008). Central Committee Resolution, April.
AKEL (2010b). Theses of the central committee to the 21st Congress, Nicosia, September.
AKEL (2011b). Subsidies and Economic Measures Given to Empower Society and the Economy, Economic and Social Studies Bureau of AKEL's Central Committee, January-February.
AKEL (2013). Political proposal for exiting the memorandum, April, Nicosia: AKEL.
AKEL (2014). Theses of AKEL's Central Committee for the Programmatic Congress, Nicosia, 15–16 February, Nicosia: AKEL.
AKEL (2015b). Theses of AKEL's Central Committee to the 22nd Congress, Nicosia, 4–7 June, Nicosia: AKEL.

Anastasiou, K. (2015). 'No Direction Home: The Promise of Soft Neoliberalism', *Theseis*, No. 132, July-September [in Greek].

Anderson, P. (2015). 'The Greek Debacle. On the crisis in Greece and Syriza's failure to resist the Eurozone', https://www.jacobinmag.com/2015/07/tspiras-syriza-euro-perry-anderson/, accessed 25 July 2015.

Andreadis, I. (2015). 'The ideological foundations of the Greek coalition government', in R. Gerodimos (Eds), *First thoughts on the 25 January 2015 election in Greece*, GPSG Pamphlet No 4, Published on 2 February 2015 by the Greek Politics Specialist Group (GPSG).

Antoniou, D. (2016). 'The Left 2015 for SYRIZA and Greece', *Kathimerini* 3 January 2016, p. 20.

Balabanidis, Y. (2015a). 'Radical Left, the Heir of Many Ancestors', *Sygxrona Themata*, 130–131 (December), pp. 46–50 [in Greek].

Bale, T. and Dunphy, R. (2011). 'In From the Cold? Left Parties and Government Involvement Since 1989', *Comparative European Politics*, 9(3), pp. 269–291.

Bruff, I. (2014). 'The Rise of Authoritarian Neoliberalism', *Rethinking Marxism*, 26(1), pp. 113–129.

Charalambous, G. and Ioannou, G. (2015). 'No Bridge over Troubled Waters: The Cypriot Left Heading the Government 2008-2013', *Capital and Class*, pp. 1–2, DOI: 10.1177/0309816815587078.

Charalambous, G. (2012b). 'AKEL and the European Union', *Greek Political Science Review*, Issue 38 [in Greek].

Christophorou, C. (2008). 'A New Communist Surprise – What's Next? Presidential Elections in the Republic of Cyprus, February 2008', *South European Society and Politics*, 13(2), pp. 217–235.

Cotta, M. (1999). 'On the Relationship Between Party and Government', N. 6/1999, Università degli Studi di Siena, Dipartimento di Scienze Storiche Giuridiche Politiche e Sociali, Via Mattioli, 10 53100 SIENA.

Crouch, C. (2004). *Post-Democracy*, Cambridge: Polity Press.

Dragasakis, Y. (2016). 'A Landmark Year', *Efimerida ton Sintakton*, 23–24 January, pp. 6–7.

Eleftheriou, C. (2015). 'The Greek Radical Left and the Crisis (2010-2015): Aspects of a Great Overturn', *Sygxrona Themata*, 130–131, December, pp. 61–73 [in Greek].

Fischer, L. and Economou, D. (2015), 'Cyprus at the Crossroads', https://www.jacobinmag.com/2015/05/cyprus-communists-SYRIZA-greece/, 26 May 2015, accessed 4 June 2015.

Gkasis, P. (2015). 'What led to the coalition government between Syriza and Independent Greeks?', in R. Gerodimos (Eds), *First thoughts on the 25 January 2015 election in Greece*, GPSG Pamphlet No 4, Published on 2 February 2015 by the Greek Politics Specialist Group (GPSG).

Glezos, M. (2015). 'Before it's too late', http://kinisienergoipolites.blogspot.com/2015/02/blog-post_574.html, Accessed 22 February.

Halikiopoulou, D. and Vasilopoulou, S. (2015). 'The middle class is the key to retaining power', in R. Gerodimos (Eds), *First thoughts on the 25 January 2015 election in Greece*, GPSG Pamphlet No 4, Published on 2 February 2015 by the Greek Politics Specialist Group (GPSG).

Hough, D. and Olsen, J. (2015). 'What happens to the left when it gains power? Look at Greece's Syriza party', https://www.washingtonpost.com/blogs/monkey-cage/wp/2015/09/02/what-happens-to-the-left-when-it-gains-power-look-at-greeces-syriza-party/?wpmm=1&wpisrc=nl_cage, Accessed 2 September 2015.

House of Representatives (2012). Proceedings from the discussions on Cyprus Agreement with the Troika, Nicosia, 15 December.

Katsourides, Y. (2012). Travelling against the Tide: The Cypriot Communist Left in the Post-1990 Era, *Perspectives on European Politics and Society*, 13 (2), pp. 187–209.

Katsourides, Y. (2016). 'Delegitimization accelerated: democracy, accountability and the troika experience in Cyprus'. *Portuguese Journal of Social Science* (forthcoming).

Kiapidou, N. (2015b). 'Europe and the 2015 Snap Greek Elections, Round 2: Results, Patterns, and Divides', https://epern.wordpress.com/2015/10/02/europe-and-the-2015-snap-greek-elections-round-2-results-patterns-and-divides/, Accessed 29 September 2015.

Kouvelakis, S. (2015). 'From the Absurd to the Tragic', https://www.jacobin-mag.com/2015/07/tsipras-syriza-greece-euro-debt/, Accessed 12 July 2015.

Kyritsis, P. (2015). 'Counterattack', *Haravgi*, 29 November 2015, p. 6.

Lapavitsas, C. (2016). 'The Year Hope was Refuted', *Efimerida ton Sintakton*, 23–24 January p. 16.

Lapavitsas, C. (2015). 'The election of the President of the Republic', http://costaslapavitsas.blogspot.com/2015/02/blog-post_18.html, Accessed on 22 February 2015.

Mavroudeas, S. (2015). 'On the Programmatic Statements of the SYRIZA-ANEL Government', https://stavrosmavroudeas.wordpress.com/2015/02/09/, Accessed 10 February 2015 [in Greek].

Monbiot, G. (2015), 'Greece is the latest battleground in the financial elite's war on democracy', http://www.theguardian.com/commentisfree/2015/jul/07/greece-financial-elite-democracy-liassez-faire-neoliberalism?CMP=share_btn_fb, accessed 2 August 2015.

Moschonas, G. (2015b). 'Critical Elections and the Interpretation of the September Elections', *Sygxrona Themata*, Issue 130–131, December, pp. 26–s28 [in Greek].

Mudde, C. (2015). *SYRIZA: The Falsification of the Populist Promise*, Thessaloniki: Epikentro [in Greek].

Mpogiopoulos, N. (2015). 'We Can only Lose our Chains', http://www.enikos.gr/mpogiopoulos/299731,Exoyme_na_xasoyme_mono_tis_alysides_ma.html, accessed 24 February 2015.

Olsen, J., Koß, M., and Hough, D. (2010). 'From Pariahs to Players? Left parties in National Governments. In J. Olsen, M. Koß and D. Hough (eds.) *Left Parties in Government*, New York: Palgrave Macmillan, pp. 1–15.

Panayiotou, A. (2014). *The First Left Presidency, 2008-2013*, Limassol: Cyprus Centre for East Mediterranean Studies [in Greek].

Papadopoulou, E. and Spourdalakis, M. (2015). 'SYRIZA's Two Months in Government: Difficulties and Challenges', http://www.globalresearch.ca/syrizas-two-months-in-government-difficulties-and-challenges/5439819, Accessed 3 April 2015.

Petras, J. (2015b). 'Syriza: Plunder, Pillage and Prostration. (How the 'Hard Left' embraces the policies of the Hard Right'. http://petras.lahaine.org/?p=2039, 15 June 2015, Accessed 22 July 2015.

Petras (2015c). 'Greek elections: January and September 2015 - From Hope to Fear and Despair', http://petras.lahaine.org/?p=2048, Accessed 1 September 2015.

Rinaldi, R. (2015). 'Statement of Resignation', http://www.e-dromos.gr/rudi-rinaldi-dhlwsh-paraithshs-apo-thn-pg-tou-syriza/, Accessed 22 July 2015.

Schmidt, V. and Thatcher, M. (2014), 'Why are neoliberal ideas so resilient in Europe's political economy?', *Critical Policy Studies*, 8(3), pp. 340–347.

Seferiades, S. (2015). 'Transforming victory to defeat', http://www.huffington-post.gr/seraphim-seferiades/-_680_b_7742920.html, Accessed 8 July 2015 [in Greek].

Sevastakis, N. (2015). 'Postscript: Thoughts on SYRIZA's Government', *Sygxrona Themata*, 130–131, December, pp. 28–31 [in Greek].

Spourdalakis, M. (2016). 'Becoming SYRIZA again', https://www.jacobinmag.com/2016/01/syriza-memorandum-troika-left-platform-tsipras-austerity-government/, accessed 1 February 2016.

Spourdalakis (2015). 'To Fight Another Day', https://www.jacobinmag.com/2015/09/syriza-election-greece-memorandum-austerity-popular-unity-tsipras/, Accessed 5 October 2015.

Spourdalakis, M. (2014), 'The Miraculous Rise of the 'Phenomenon SYRIZA'', *International Critical Thought*, 4(3), pp. 354–366.

Sygkelos, Y. (2015). 'A Critical Analysis of the Greek Referendum of July 2015', *Contemporary Southeastern Europe*, 2(2), pp. 1–6.

SYRIZA Youth (2015). Regarding the Voting of the Third Memorandum', http://rproject.gr/article/anakoinosi-tis-neolaias-syriza-gia-tin-psifisi-toy-tritoy-mnimonioy, Accessed 13 August 2015.

SYRIZA (2015). 'A Blueprint of the Government Programme', August 2015, http://www.avgi.gr/documents/10179/0/%CE%A3%CE%A7%CE%95%CE%94%CE%99%CE%9F%20%CE%A0%CE%A1%CE%9F%CE%93%CE%A1%CE%91%CE%9C%CE%9C%CE%91%CE%A4%CE%9F%CE%A3%20%CE%A3%CE%A5%CE%A1%CE%99%CE%96%CE%91/b29e5a3e-41b8-4a17-b7cc-caba9d0e68af, Accessed 23 September 2015.

SYRIZA (2014). 'The Thessaloniki Programme', http://www.syriza.gr/article/id/57965/OMILIA-TOY-PROEDROY-TOY-SYRIZA-ALEKSH-TSIPRA-STO-SYNEDRIAKO-KENTRO-I.-BELLIDHS-ThESSALONIKH-13-9-2014. html#.VnrVX8tukdU, Accessed 15 September 2014.

Teperoglou, E. (2015). 'The sleeping giant dreams up a new coalition', in R. Gerodimos (Eds), *First thoughts on the 25 January 2015 election in Greece*, GPSG Pamphlet No 4, Published on 2 February 2015 by the Greek Politics Specialist Group (GPSG).

Traynor, I. (2015). 'SYRIZA's historic win puts Greece on collision course with Europe', http://www.theguardian.com/world/2015/jan/25/syriza-historic-win-greece-european-union-austerity, Accessed 26 January.

Tsipras, A. (2016). 'One Year Left. One Year of Struggle. We Move On', Speech delivered on the anniversary of one year in government, Athens, 24 January, https://left.gr/news/anoihti-politiki-sygkentrosi-toy-syriza-me-omiliti-ton-al-tsipra-1-hronos-aristera-1-hronos, accessed 25 January 2015.

Tsipras, A. (2015). Policy Statement, 8 February 2015, http://www.primeminister.gov.gr/2015/02/08/13322, accessed 9 February 2015 [in Greek].

Tsirbas, Y. (2015). 'The January 2015 Parliamentary Election in Greece: Government Change, Partial Punishment and Hesitant Stabilization', *South European Society and Politics*, http://dx.doi.org/10.1080/13608746.2015.1088428.

Vernardakis, C. (2015). 'The Party, the Government and the State: The Challenges for SYRIZA', http://www.vernardakis.gr/article.php?id=599, Accessed 22 February 2015 [in Greek].

CHAPTER 7

Conclusions: What to Do?

Abstract This concluding chapter underlines how the two parties' radical identity is at risk because of their decision to "manage capitalism"—an act that prioritizes maintaining power over the parties' social vision. It addresses a number of important issues consequent to their decision to pursue government, and relevant to their handling of the executive branch. The chapter also highlights some possible implications for future research on radical Left parties.

Keywords Radical Left parties • AKEL • SYRIZA • Government participation • De-radicalization • Policy impact • Alternatives

One month after the collapse of the Lehmann Brothers Bank in autumn 2008, on 18 October the *Economist* issued a front-cover warning about a liberal world order: "capitalism at bay." Marx and Keynes rose to the forefront, as several countries nationalized their banks using taxpayer money to save them from bankruptcy. Social movements and popular protests shook the globe—for example, the Occupy movement in North America and the Indignados in Europe. Like in Latin America some years earlier, Left populism loomed large, and radical Left parties (RLPs) saw an opportunity to present their vision to the people. Now, eight years after the Left's attempt at governance, it became clear that capitalism was too resilient to be replaced, yet also dangerously unstable. However, the real

© The Editor(s) (if applicable) and The Author(s) 2016
Y. Katsourides, *Radical Left Parties in Government*,
DOI 10.1057/978-1-137-58841-8_7

threat— once again pointed out by the *Economist* (12 December 2015)— this time was the extreme and radical Right. This was not unrelated to the way the radical Left responded to the ongoing economic crisis, particularly when they were at the head of a government.

This book has examined two RLPs—the Progressive Party of Working People (AKEL) and the Coalition of the Radical Left (SYRIZA)— that achieved executive office during the years 2008–2016, focusing on their trajectories from opposition party to governing party, and how their policies responded to the challenge of government, especially amid a huge economic crisis. Their degree of de-radicalization was a crucial issue in this investigation, particularly under the impact of government-opposition dynamics. If one thing stands out, it is that the Left in government has never been the subject of easy discussion among leftists. This is directly related to the fact that any Left attempt at radically transforming society has been a painful experience with numerous retreats, defeats, diversions, and disappointments.

Nevertheless, it is imperative that the debates on this topic make meaningful comparisons (i.e., examination of comparable cases) while incorporating enough abstraction to avoid irrelevant generalizations (Spourdalakis 2016). This book has tried to do that; it has taken into consideration the various objective and subjective conditions and histories of the two countries and parties while situating them within the overall context of radical Left politics.

Although AKEL and SYRIZA operate in two separate countries with many similar cultural and historical characteristics, the parties differ significantly in terms of ideology, party organization, and history. Nonetheless, they reveal considerable similarities with regard to their experiences in office. Both parties' government experience appears to confirm a popular thesis in the emerging literature on RLPs (at least on governing RLPs), which posits an inability to execute their alternative policies. This study also has found that conventional political science tools, those used to study mainstream political party families, are suited to their study as well.

The Left and Government and the Left in Government

When in 1902 Lenin famously asked, "*What is to be done?*," he probably did not expect that the question would trouble leftist parties well into the twenty-first century. This book has examined that question as well as others in relation to the experiences of the two parties under study. A *first* important question is *why* they aim to enter government, with the common answer (Olsen et al. 2010) being that RLPs believe that incumbency is the only way to remain politically relevant in contemporary politics. Moreover, many RLPs have lost voters by remaining in opposition and therefore are skeptical of claims that they will garner more votes by staying there (Bale and Dunphy 2011: 282). Wahl (2010: 92) suggests that their widespread movement towards government participation has been spurred by discontent with their minority support status—the worst of all worlds in that they have responsibility for government policy without the power to affect it.

Currently, it is common for RLPs to join coalition governments in an effort to counter neo-liberalism and to steer the governmental centre of gravity to the Left—objectives they achieve by making incremental advances through their own policy agenda and by acting as the left-wing conscience of social democrats (e,g., see Daiber 2010). The two RLPs under study here were and are no different: AKEL first, and SYRIZA later, carved a governing path with the intention to influence policy decisions. AKEL prioritized the Cyprus Problem, whereas SYRIZA emphasized an end to austerity policies. Because of the two parties' prior exclusion from governing, they appeared distinct and fresh, untainted by past experiences. Therefore, when they decided to pursue full participation in government, they were in an advantageous position compared to other parties.

For AKEL, already a large party, governing by means of its leader was the next logical step to its earlier participation in coalition governments. In a society where ideology had long ago become secondary, the prospect of full participation offered tangible benefits for the party's diverse voters. It was the glue that united them all towards a common goal. Focusing on solving the Cyprus Problem enabled the party leadership to justify the absence of any radical societal transformation on its agenda. In the case of SYRIZA, the party was presented with a unique opportunity to claim power: it promised to honour the people's mandate to cancel the austerity policies of previous governments. In a rapidly changing environment, had SYRIZA not taken the opportunity to present a governing proposal, it likely would have receded into insignificance.

A *second* and directly associated matter concerns their readiness to govern. Both AKEL and SYRIZA turned out to be ill-equipped for the task. Either because of naivety or lack of preparation, both parties were sorely mistaken in their expectation that administering the state would be "business as usual." Once in office, their policies were not always clear; in fact they were often vague and conflicting, not the least because they wanted to reconcile what was actually irreconcilable (e.g., their wish for radical transformation with acceptance of fundamental capitalist norms and processes). As a consequence, they were perceived as incapable of governing, and both AKEL and SYRIZA were so accused. In fact, any proposals that countered existing frames and paradigms were proclaimed as inapplicable or potentially catastrophic—for example, SYRIZA's intention to cancel part of the debt and AKEL's proposal for a wealth tax.

As the literature suggests, RLPs have had little experience in governing, and when they do attain office, they seek to prove that they are up to the task. Moreover, they tend to loudly publicize any measures their partys' proposed successfully or managed to implement. For example, AKEL published several special leaflets detailing all government achievements (as it saw them) and delivered them door to door throughout Cyprus (e.g., see AKEL 2011b). This was also a part of a strategy to convince the membership and voters that any compromises were made for strategic reasons. This also was related to the so-called "blame game"—attributing inefficiencies, rightfully or wrongly, to greater powers, usually outside the country.

The *third* and probably more important issue refers to how party policy becomes affected by governing, and what RLPs actually achieve once in government. This subject touches on the fundamental question of the parties' radical character, because governing may provide influence but also risks de-radicalization.

Although RLPs are increasingly keen to participate in government, their actual impact while in government has been minimal (March 2012: 315). The radical Left can point to only modest reforms attained while in office—for example, incremental increases in welfare and employment benefits, the dilution of privatization and marketization, some increases in governmental subsidies and regulation (Daiber and Kulke 2010: 17)— hardly a "radical" reformulation of neo-liberalism. Even in the few cases where the radical Left has been the dominant party in government, as in Cyprus and Greece, there has been little indication that government policy has differed from that of left-wing social democratic parties; this is so despite a greater emphasis on the states' role in the economy and greater skepticism towards the Euro-Atlantic institutions (March 2008: 14). SYRIZA's interpretation of the crisis as humanitarian, for example, is closer to traditional social democracy.

SYRIZA and AKEL have not enacted any structural reforms that carry beyond their short terms of government participation. On some of the most important issues (e.g., joining or remaining in the Eurozone, participation in NATO by Greece, and austerity measures), neither party was able to turn the tide. Both parties were largely exhausted by their defensive strategies aimed at preventing the worst. The real question therefore is whether any of their measures or reforms would be reversed as soon as there was a shift in power. In Cyprus, where the government already has changed, not even one of the most modest reforms has remained in effect; however, it must be noted that this process had been previously set in motion by the AKEL government itself during late 2011 when a "domestic Memorandum" was applied.

It appears that the anticipation to govern and governing have had a moderating effect on both parties' policies, albeit at different stages and at different rates. In opposition the two parties' rhetoric and policy positions were more radical, becoming more compromising when governing was in view or when they actually governed. The fact that the government-opposition dynamics played an important role in their strategy (i.e., policy) confirms the hypothesis that governmentalism exerts a moderating effect on RLPs too.

The two parties campaigned for votes promising (1) a more egalitarian programme; and (2) a programme that they could effectively negotiate within the sphere of Eurozone mechanisms, institutions, political dynamics, and geopolitical surroundings. They failed on both goals, particularly SYRIZA, and were forced to make a series of compromises in order to comply with external (i.e., European Union, EU) and internal (i.e., media and other parties') pressures. To this end both parties concentrated on shorter term pragmatic proposals at the expense of any plans for transformation. This action–reaction highlighted the inconsistencies in their policies—for example, the normative ideological goals versus the practical short-term demands of governing, the anti-capitalist culture of protest defining their inner-party core supporters and expressed in internal documents versus their compromising strategies, the critique of contemporary capitalism that includes anti-systemic characteristics while managing the same system.

Both parties adopted a pragmatic policy even while trumpeting phony leftist rhetoric and feigning resistance. In this way party leaders tried to rationalize what they described as "realistic and pragmatic compromises." Of course, such tactics only served to strip leftist phraseology of any real meaning, indicating at the same time the severe limitations placed on RLPs (Petras 2015b). Once in office, both parties were constrained by the practical demands of governing and had to take actions that proved unpopular with their supporters. Both parties sacrificed their ideological beliefs to gain political effectiveness.

Marxism was valuable as rhetoric and as an explanatory tool but of little use in designing public policy. Indeed, while the two parties were in office, Left social democratic programmes were at the forefront—for example, Keynesian economics, an emphasis on full employment, and public ownership. However, in the EU today not even Keynes is accepted. Therefore, deprived of their pathfinders (i.e., Marx and Keynes), as Sassoon (1997) argued for left social democrats, they adopted a defensive strategy, hoping to mitigate and even reverse neo-liberal policies—as did many other RLPs (Bale and Dunphy 2011: 278; Daiber and Kulke 2010: 9).

Their strategies were defined by the following principles:

- Market forces can be regulated but not eliminated, and this regulation must take place in a coordinated European frame.
- Public spending must take cuts where appropriate.
- The welfare state can be defended but not extended, and even sometimes can be trimmed
- Privatization cannot be avoided and is sometimes acceptable.
- Equality must be a goal but in compliance with productivity and competiveness
- The power of international financial institutions must be contained via international agreements, not unilateral state policies
- The EU must change in a more social direction, but it is accepted as a place where constant battles take place.

All these suggest de-radicalization. Nevertheless, both AKEL and SYRIZA insisted that this "defensive" fight was meant to protect the social democratic state but did not preclude a more radical (but undefined) "socialist" agenda in the future.

A *fourth* issue concerns the direct impact on RLPs of governing, including their electoral fortunes. It appears that although RLPs believe that governing was a necessary and often unavoidable step, these parties suffered electoral losses, schisms, and divisions as a result. Party unity was tested in government, and the organizational tradition of each party, as well as the political and party culture in each country, became crucial,

especially in relation to splinter groups and new parties' potential for survival. It seems that governing tended to decrease a party's ability to mobilize and to initiate protest. In sum, government participation seemed to
cost too much for most RLPs. The losses were particularly severe where
there were alternative Left (or Right) protest parties that attracted dissatis-
fied voters (March 2008: 14) but even without other Left alternatives, as
AKEL's electoral performance in 2016 showed.

Two factors were especially important in terms of how severely governing impacted the two parties: first, the (non)existence of other Left parties that could benefit from their failure and/or de-radicalization; second,
each party's ideological and organizational traditions and the resultant
ability to manage turmoil. On both factors, AKEL was in a more favourable position.

In Greece, the trauma of taking over power proved politically chasten-
ing for SYRIZA, and the party suffered numerous disputes and divisions
that led to major internal crises. Many members, as well as constituent
organizations, left the party during this period; some of them created a
new party (LAE). Although not electorally costly to the party, at least
then, SYRIZA was clearly becoming an office-seeking party rather than a
programmatically pure one; thus, it risked becoming just like other mainstream parties. AKEL, on the other hand, did not suffer any splits during
or after its governing tenure; however, the party failed to reach the 30 %
psychological electoral threshold in three consecutive elections following its exit from government. The party polled approximately 27 % in
the presidential elections of 2013 and the European elections of 2014
before scoring its lowest ever result (25.67 %) in the most recent parliamentary elections (May 2016), evidently paying the price for governing
participation.

Clearly, disappointed and disillusioned party members may well have
looked to other Left parties. Here, AKEL's advantage is clear: in Cyprus
there are still no "Left counterbalances"—there was no party to the left of
AKEL. The only check and balance to AKEL came from its more rightist
flanks, and although disappointed AKEL voters have moved away, they
have not yet realigned, at least not the majority of them. SYRIZA, in
contrast, was not the only Left party in Greece, and it has suffered losses
as a result.

Also crucial to a party's ability to respond to upsets are its history and
its organizational tradition; here again SYRIZA was disadvantaged in comparison to AKEL. SYRIZA was established 24 years ago, and those years

have been marked by continuous factionalism and ideologically loaded debates. As of mid-2016, the party is still very vulnerable to significant political changes and internal developments. AKEL, with its strict Leninist organization, lack of ideological discussion and/or debate, and an inward party culture, has absorbed its disappointment relatively cost-free.

Another issue relates to the party's political stance after it leaves office. Clearly, we are speaking only of AKEL, because SYRIZA remains in government. Some studies (e.g., Olsen et al. 2010) suggest that RLPs tend to re-ideologize once they leave office; this was so in AKEL's case. Although the party became more radical in the second half of its governing tenure, this was not without reason. AKEL radicalized when it was evident that it stood no chance of reelection and when, subsequently, in the opposition. More than three years after the change in government, AKEL still struggled to shake off the consequences of its five-year presidency. Many people blamed the party for the bail-in agreement and the downturn of the economy. Still, with the passage of time, AKEL probably will find it easier to deploy its policies and regain the loyalty of its voters; this is already evident. That the party has re-ideologized is obvious (e.g., AKEL's proposal for renationalization), but its new programme is not yet widely accepted.

SYRIZA, on the other hand, has not returned to opposition; as such, there is not yet the empirical evidence required to analyze its position. The party's path in government clearly suggests de-radicalization. Moreover, SYRIZA is in danger of falling into earlier political practices, which were confined to calculations of positions held in the leadership and subsequent symbolic advances. Their decision, in the September 2015 elections, to form a coalition with Independent Greeks (ANEL) instead the Pan-Hellenic Socialist Movement (PASOK, or Potami) might suggest that SYRIZA's leadership consciously chose to build a populist leftist party, following in the footsteps of A. Papandreou's PASOK: enraged in rhetoric but realistic in practice (Mudde 2015: 101).

This study also reveals that *timing* matters. The international–external context plays an important role—that is, the world situation when the party took on governing responsibilities as well as when it stepped down. Whereas initially the economic crisis seemed to favour an RLP agenda, this turned out to be a much more complicated undertaking, as the SYRIZA case clearly reveals. SYRIZA was elected to office amid the economic crisis with the promise to end austerity and restore peoples' dignity; however, after many struggles it found itself forced to capitulate to EU demands.

Elected during the crisis and unwilling to resign, the SYRIZA government found itself in the middle of a "perfect storm" without an escape plan.

AKEL had already taken the reins of government when the crisis hit Cyprus and, because of the timing of the elections, was lucky to have stepped down before the actual effects of the EU Memorandum were felt. Consequently, and although accused of having played a large role in the economic disaster and the resulting austerity, it now found room for re-radicalizing. Overall, therefore, although it would seem that periods of turbulence would benefit radical Left projects, this study reveals it to be otherwise.

In Search of Alternatives

This study's investigation into the governing experiences of AKEL and SYRIZA shows that these parties resemble all other European RLPs in their inability to present and to promote a feasible governing plan. Both SYRIZA and AKEL, albeit in varying degrees, submitted to the paramount logic of governing within the capitalist frame and, particularly, SYRIZA within the confines of neo-liberalism. Once in government they were unable to promote their alternative policies, which increasingly made them look like all other parties. Moreover, they seemed to become quite politically disoriented.

Not only AKEL and SYRIZA, but also RLPs in general, appear incapable of articulating a concrete set of alternative proposals—that is, actual policies that offer solutions to existing problems. Because the RPLs cannot outline a viable programme to achieve their alternative vision for society, and thus challenge capitalism and neo-liberalism, they are merely forced to oppose them. Regardless of the specific reasons, it was the absence of concrete proposals compatible with their ideological legacies that forced AKEL and SYRIZA into mere management of everyday politics. The result of this was that the RLP claim to be a vehicle of long-term societal transformation was compromised. Their choice to "manage capitalism" shifted the stakes from the parties' social vision to the issue of maintaining power.

For the foreseeable future, socialist change appears to have been put on hold, legitimizing in this way the current compromises. Communists and radical leftists, of which AKEL and SYRIZA are very good examples, tend to focus more on improving bourgeois democracy than transforming society. They were essentially aligning their theories to their practices, much as the German social democrats did in Bad Godesberg in 1959. In the words of Poulantzas: "[W]e are waiting for the Great Night by spending the day making reforms" (cited in Mpelantis 2014: 89). Socialism seems to have no special weight in the RLPs' politics; in these parties' aspirations to govern, it has been relegated to second place. Their participation in government only serves to further their incorporation into the system, not to change of the system.

Their abstract and sparse reference to socialism merely disguises their de-radicalization, and this employment of a communist imaginary serves to maintain useful electoral linkages with their past. As history has shown, earlier leftist attempts at governing in South Europe led to no social change because they, and the RLPs in this study, chose a contractual relationship with capitalism instead of rupture. Both AKEL and SYRIZA promoted themselves as parties that combined social struggle and governance; however, this was easier said than done. Left governmentalism as a means in itself threatens to negate the substantial differences between radical leftists and social democrats. Confining their efforts to humanizing capitalism could prove the end to their socialist plan.

Answering important strategic questions remains a challenge for RLPs, one they must meet or they are doomed to remain a well-equipped oppositional party but not a governing one. Governing in the current global and European context requires a realistic plan that takes into consideration the balance of power not only within each country but also within the EU. Whether this can be achieved in the EU, as some communist parties and authors argue (e.g., Mudde 2015: 74), remains to be seen. The EU is not the ideal place for socialist ideologies, moderate or radical. It is not supportive of more economic regulation, a more encompassing welfare state, or Keynesian deficit spending. Perhaps the biggest challenge for RLPs, then, is to develop a distinct vision relevant to contemporary Europe (March 2012: 336). This must examine whether one radical government alone can change the EU's neo-liberal direction.

Although the economic crisis offered an opening and an opportunity for the radical Left, it also exposed its ideological and political shortcomings. The radical Left seems to be experiencing an identity crisis, similar to that of the traditional communist Left following the dissolution of the socialist bloc in 1991. At present, the radical Left lacks a distinct ideological-programmatic formula in the domain of economic and social policy. Their agenda resembles the social democratic agenda of the 1960s and 1970s (Mudde 2015: 135).

The central strategic problem is moving from an acknowledged position of strategic defence of the Keynesian welfare state to a more proactive transformation of capitalism (March 2012: 337). In truth, this is an old dilemma, but it is highlighted more than ever because of the ongoing crisis. In the words of D. Enkelmann (2016), president of the Rosa Luxemburg Foundation: "the radical Left needs a new, common narrative that would resonate both with peoples' demands" and socialist ideology.

The question of narrative highlights one of the major failings in government of the two RLPs under study. Narrative requires both a sense of orientation and a way of talking to people; it requires a clear vision of the future. This probably means a need to rewrite the agenda, to rewrite the narrative of the past and especially for the future. It also means the necessity to coalesce around a number of key agenda items. For example, they might work towards tackling inequality and forging a workable synthesis of inspirational movement politics within an effective election-winning machine.

Still, even if there is agreement on "what is to be done" (i.e., the famous Lenin axiom), the even thornier question is whether there is anyone to do it. This challenge relates directly to the problem of agency: "[A]re there social and political forces, inspiring ideas, or sufficiently resourceful actors who might offer Europeans [an] alternative and at the same time realistic policy proposals?" (Offe 2015: vii). It certainly has not helped the Left's cause that leftist governments have been in power in two of the most crisis-hit nations (i.e., Greece, Cyprus) and exposed the gap in their pre-campaign rhetoric and their actual governing performance.

Further Implications

Left parties always find governing difficult, but is this not true for all political parties? In other words, it appears that parties of the Left behave in remarkably similar ways to parties of other ideologies. Bale and Dunphy (2011: 286) suggest a reevaluation of Leftist parties, positing that what has historically divided RLPs from social democratic parties has had less importance recently. If true, this means that the governing experience of socialist and social democratic parties (and of SYRIZA and AKEL) can suggest the likely trajectory of other governing RLPs. Moreover, as RLPs that are aiming to govern have become more mainstream, the conventional tools of political analysis (e.g., the "vote-office-policy" framework) are suitable for their analysis too. Furthermore, RLPs' practice in government creates the theoretical framework for their future evaluation and analysis; it is possible that predetermined Marxist ideological schemes and guidelines often prove inadequate.

While the previously discussed implications relate to theoretical issues, there also are practical repercussions. The inability of governing RLPs to radically change the societies within which they operate once in power affects the fortunes of other radical parties. If AKEL's case did not affect the rest of the European radical Left, SYRIZA clearly has already done damage (Mudde 2015: 27). SYRIZA proposed a bailout without austerity, despite the fact that European elites consistently rejected this as not an option (ibid., p. 39)—an action that has hurt the European anti-austerity movements and parties (e.g., Podemos). The claim that the Eurozone's confines are adjustable, and that the tactics focused on a consensual mood and pursuit of institutional negotiations at the EU level, are inspired by assumptions previously defended by SYRIZA.

Thus far, SYRIZA also has had a positive effect. For example, other RLPs—that is, the Portuguese Bloco and the Portuguese Communist Party (PCP), following their electoral increase in the national elections— have agreed to support a governing coalition with the Socialist Party in an attempt to change the austerity agenda. On the other hand, this might be interpreted as a process of de-radicalization if we assume these parties also will follow SYRIZA's path. SYRIZA's win, and AKEL's before that, likely – will boost the spirits and success of similar parties in Europe. Their success will put pressure on those more established RLPs that have not been able to significantly increase their political fortunes (e.g., the Left Party in France and the Dutch SP). This also could lead to more left-wing insurgencies within the social democratic parties (Mudde 2015: 40).

It may be argued that Cyprus is too small to matter, and that the crisis had not yet begun when AKEL assumed power, and that the Cypriot communists never symbolized the movement-like dynamism of the anti-austerity march that SYRIZA contributed to creating. Therefore, the trajectory that SYRIZA will follow until and/or when it eventually ends its government tenure, which points to full emulation of previous PASOK's practices, is anticipated with great interest. The September 2015 election was probably the last that SYRIZA could win purely on the basis of the failure of the other parties. Whenever new elections take place, SYRIZA will be judged on its own merits, and the party will not be able to blame any failure on previous office holders.

For the time being, more questions are posed than answers provided. The balance of power between countries and between political/social forces continues to be the actual benchmark against which all intentions are measured. Given all these, the classic question "what is to be done," or better "what can be done," will probably continue to plague contemporary RLPs.

BIBLIOGRAPHY

AKEL (2011b). Subsidies and Economic Measures Given to Empower Society and the Economy, Economic and Social Studies Bureau of AKEL's Central Committee, January-February.
Bale, T. and Dunphy, R. (2011). 'In From the Cold? Left Parties and Government Involvement Since 1989', Comparative European Politics, 9(3), pp. 269–291.
Daiber, B. and Kulke, R. (2010). 'Introduction', in Daiber, B. (Eds.) The Left in Government. Latin America and Europe Compared, Brussels: Rosa Luxemburg Foundation, pp. 7–20.
Enkelmann, D. (2016). 'The Perception that Tsipras is a Traitor will Damage the Entire Left', Interview in Efimerida ton Sintakton, 23–24 January, p. 11.
March, L. (2012). 'Problems and Perspectives of Contemporary European Radical Left Parties: Chasing a Lost World or Still a World to Win?', International Critical Thought, 2(3), pp. 314–339.
March, L. (2008). Contemporary Far Left Parties in Europe – From Marxism to the Mainstream? Friedrich Ebert Foundation, November 2008, Berlin: library. fes.de/pdf-files/id/ipa/05818.pdf.
Mudde, C. (2015). SYRIZA: The Falsification of the Populist Promise, Thessaloniki: Epikentro [in Greek].
Mpelantis, D. (2014). The Left and Power: The "Democratic Way" to Socialism, Athens: Topos [in Greek].
Offe, K. (2015). Europe Entrapped, Cambridge: Polity Press.
Olsen, J., Koß, M., and Hough, D. (2010). 'From Pariahs to Players? Left parties in National Governments. In J. Olsen, M. Koß and D. Hough (eds.) Left Parties in Government, New York: Palgrave Macmillan, pp. 1–15.
Petras, J. (2015b). 'Syriza: Plunder, Pillage and Prostration. (How the 'Hard Left' embraces the policies of the Hard Right'. http://petras.lahaine.org/?p=2039, 15 June 2015, Accessed 22 July 2015.
Sassoon, D. (Ed) (1997). Looking Left, London: I. B. Tauris.
Spourdalakis, M. (2016). 'Becoming SYRIZA again', https://www.jacobinmag.com/2016/01/syriza-memorandum-troika-left-platform-tsipras-austerity-government/, accessed 1 February 2016.
Wahl, A. (2010). 'To be in Office, but not in Power: Left Parties in the Squeeze between Peoples' Expectations and an Unfavourable Balance of Power', in Daiber, B. (Eds.) The Left in Government. Latin America and Europe Compared, Brussels: Rosa Luxemburg Foundation, pp. 85–94.

BIBLIOGRAPHY

Alavanos, A. (2008). Speech at the 5th Party Congress, Athens, 7 February 2008, http://www.syn.gr/gr/keimeno.php?id=8935, accessed 21 September 2015.

Antifascism Europa (2013). European Antifascist Manifesto, Feb. 12, 2013: antifascismeuropa.org/manifesto/en.

Balabanidis, Y. (2015b). *Eurocommunism: From the Communist to the Radical European Left*, Athens: Polis [in Greek].

Close, D. H. (1993). (Ed.), *The Greek Civil War 1943-1950*, London: Routledge.

Eleftheriou, C. (2015). 'The Greek Radical Left and the Crisis (2010-2015): Aspects of a Great Overturn', *Sygxrona Themata*, Issue 130–131, December, pp. 61–73 [in Greek].

Kathimerini (2015). 'Greek Government Shelves Parallel Programme', http://www.ekathimerini.com/204443/article/ekathimerini/news/greek-government-shelves-parallel-program, 18 December 2015, accessed 20 December 2015.

Poulantzas, N. [1970] (2006). *Fascism and Dictatorship*, Athens: Themelio.

© The Editor(s) (if applicable) and The Author(s) 2016
Y. Katsourides, *Radical Left Parties in Government*,
DOI 10.1057/978-1-137-58841-8

INDEX

Note: Page numbers with "n" denote notes.

© The Editor(s) (if applicable) and The Author(s) 2016   161
Y. Katsourides, *Radical Left Parties in Government*,
DOI 10.1057/978-1-137-58841-8

Kathimerini (newspaper), 126, 131
Katsambekis, Giorgos, 49, 95, 97,
 99–101, 103, 105
Katsiaounis, Rolandos, 107
Katsourides, Yiannos, 11, 16, 72–4,
 76, 77, 79–80, 82, 85–7, 110,
 111, 131, 137–9
Katz, Richard, 17, 32, 38, 80
Kautksy, Karl, 34
Kenneth, Janda, 17
Ker-Lindsay, James, 75, 89n1
Keynes, 118–25, 128, 145, 150
Keynesian economic policy, mode, 5
Kiapidou, Nikoleta, 104, 126
Kitschelt, Herbert, 38
KKE. *See* Greek Communist Party
 (KKE)
KKE-ES (Communist Party of the
 Interior), Reformist Left, 36, 47,
 51, 65
Kolokasides, Yiannakis, 106, 109, 110
Kompsopoulos, Jannis, 11, 12, 95, 98
Koß, Michael, 2, 17, 18, 25, 27, 41,
 44, 117, 142, 147, 152
Kosovo War, 53
Kotsaka, Theodora, 48, 50, 95, 96
Kotsonopoulos, Loudovikos, 48, 50,
 95, 96
Kouvelakis, Stathis, 13, 94, 124
Kouvelis, Photis, 54, 55
Kriesi, H., 36
Kulke, Roland, 2, 16, 21n1, 40, 148,
 150
Kyprianou, Spyros (President), 107
Kyritsis, Pambis, 135

L
Labour governments, 31
Ladrech, Robert, 11, 85
Lafazanis, Panayiotis, 59, 125
Lamprinou, Katerina, 94, 96, 103
Lane, Jean-Erik, 3

Lapavitsas, Costas, 14, 98, 120, 124
Latin America, 21n1, 122, 145
Lavelle, Ashley, 14
Laver, Michael, 17, 18, 109
Left
 communist, 1, 2, 15, 28, 29, 33,
 48, 154
 Europeanism, 64, 104, 137
 governance, 2
 libertarianism, 39
 parties, 1, 2, 5, 10, 16, 17, 20, 27,
 29, 37–40, 45, 48, 49, 65, 86,
 117, 145, 151, 155
 Party, 2, 7, 8, 10, 11, 18, 20, 48,
 51, 52, 59, 61, 65, 76, 111,
 151, 156
 party family, 10, 11, 18, 20
 radical, 1–11, 14–16, 18–20, 27,
 32, 37–41, 45, 49, 53, 54, 56,
 59, 61, 64, 86, 93, 95, 97,
 111, 117–39, 145, 146, 148,
 153–6
 Reformist, 47, 48, 51, 58
 socialist parties, 3
 strategies, 2
Left, Communist, 1, 2, 15, 28, 29, 33,
 48, 154
Left Current *(Aristero Revma)*, 53,
 59, 63
Left Platform, 59, 64, 98, 128
Left, Socialist, 8
Lehmann Brothers Bank, 145
Lenin, 61, 146, 155
Leninist model/strategy, theory, 28
Leontios (Archbishop), 74, 75,
 107, 118
Leventis, Giorgos, 74
Liberal democracy, 3, 5, 16, 34, 39,
 89, 105
Lightfoot, Simon, 9–11
Lisbon Treaty, 87
Luxemburg, Rosa, 41, 61, 155
Lyrintzis, Costas, 14, 45, 48–50, 96

M

Maastricht Treaty, 11, 52, 53, 62
Macedonian question, 62
Mair, Peter, 3, 9, 17, 20, 32, 38, 80,
  85, 89, 108
Makarios, Archbishop, 74, 107
Mallinson, William, 89n1
Maoist Communist Organization of
  Greece (KOE), 64
Maoist Greek Communist
  Organization (KOE), 125
Marantzidis, Nicos, 61
March, Luke, 2–6, 10, 13–14, 16, 29,
  37, 39, 65, 148, 151, 154–6
Marginalization, political, 29, 46, 138
Marioulas, Julian, 45, 50, 51, 58–62,
  65, 74
Marshall Plan, 102
Marxism, 31, 32, 58, 71, 81–3, 105,
  150
Marx, Karl, 27, 58, 145, 150
Mavris, Yannis, 46–7, 97
Mavroudeas, Stavros, 122
May 1968, 33, 36
May Day 1944, 118
Memorandum, 2010, 49
Memorandums
  Cyprus, 13
  Greece, 13, 94, 95, 102, 103
Metapolitefsi
  Late, 49
  Third Greek Republic, 48
Mexico, 41
Meynaud, Jean, 47
Mikhaylov, Slava, 14
Miliband, Ralph, 39
Militant Workers (META), 60
Modernization, 29, 31, 35, 49, 50,
  52, 61, 62, 83
Monbiot, George, 121
Monti, Mario, 13
Moschonas, Gerasimos, 2, 97, 98,
  105, 124

Moscow, communist parties, 34, 35,
  37, 47
Mouzelis, Nicos, 30
Mpalafas, Yiannis, 51, 52, 54, 59, 61,
  62, 64
Mpelantis, Demetris, 28, 30, 36, 58,
  64, 154
Mpenas, Takis, 47
Mpogiopoulos, Nicos, 122
Mudde, Cas, 2–5, 37, 123, 124, 129,
  152, 154, 156
Muller, Wolfgang, 16

N

National Democratic Change, 47
Nationalist Independent Greeks Party
  (ANEL), 96, 97, 104, 118–20,
  125, 152
National Organization of Cypriot
  Fighters (EOKA), 74, 107
National Resistance Memorial, 118
NATO, anti, 5, 31, 32, 50, 74, 75, 78,
  84, 87, 122, 129, 149
Nazi, occupation, 46
Nea Dimokratia (New
  Democracy-ND), 48, 119, 120
Negri, Antonio, 61
Neo-liberalism, disciplinary, 12
Netherlands, 8, 38
New Labour Party, 30
New Left/Left Socialist Waves, 3
Nicos Poulantzas Research
  Institute, 60
Nikolakakis, Nicolaos, 104
Nikolakopoulos, E., 97,
9/11 Terrorist Attacks, 63
Non-Leftist Left (NLL), 4
Nordic Green Left Party of the
  European Left, 10
North America, 145
Norway, 8, 38, 39
Nuclear, anti, 34

Red-Green Network, 57
Renewal Wing, 59, 63
Renewed Democratic Socialist
   Movement (ADISOK), 76, 77
Renewing Modernizing Movement of
   the Left (AEKA), 53
Republican Turkish Party (CTP),
   111, 130
Republic of Cyprus, 74, 75, 109
Rinaldi, Rudi, 125
Roder, Knut, 4, 9, 10, 14
Rommerskirchen, Charlotte, 13, 16
Rosa Luxemburg Foundation, 155
Russian Revolution, 3, 28, 72, 82
Russia, October Revolution, 72

S
Sant Cassia, Paul, 106
Sartori, Giovanni, 20
Sassoon, Donald, 29–37, 39, 150
Schafer, Armin, 12
Scharpf, Fritz, 12
Schmidt, Vivien, 14, 118
Second International, 29
Seferiades, Seraphim, 122, 124
Sevastakis, Nikolas, 120, 129
17N, 63
Simerini (newspaper), 130
Simitis, Costas, 49, 50, 61, 63
Single European Act, 11
Smith, Rand, 30
Social democracy, Marxist, 28
Social democrats, 2, 14, 29, 30, 33,
   36, 46, 65, 81, 147, 150, 154
Social Europe, 10, 64–6, 87
Socialism, democratic road to, 28, 36
Socialist bloc, 29, 32, 37, 51, 64, 71,
   76, 84, 105, 150
Socialist International, 39
Socialist parties, South European, 3,
   27, 29–33, 37
Sodara, M.J., 33

Soviet bloc, era, 1, 37, 78
Soviet Union, 33, 51, 65, 72, 75
Spain, 13, 29, 33, 34, 118
Spanish Civil War, 72
Spanish Socialist Workers Party
   (PSOE), 32
Sparsis, Mikis, 82
Spourdalakis, Michalis, 15, 32, 39, 46,
   48, 49, 51–2, 54, 55, 58, 63, 66,
   94, 95, 99–101, 120, 122, 124,
   127, 128, 146
Spyropoulou, Vivian, 99
Stalinism, 34, 78, 81
The State, Power, Socialism, 36
Stavrakakis, Yannis, 49, 95, 97,
   99–101, 103, 105
Stephanou, Stephanos, 138
Strom, Kaare, 16, 17
Strongos, Paul, 72
Sygkelos Yannis, 123
Synaspismos
   5th Congress, 54
   2003 Programmatic, 53, 63
   Youth Organization, 60
SYRIZA, 4, 6, 11, 14, 15, 18–20, 32,
   45–66, 86, 93–106, 118–29,
   140n4, 146–56
SYRIZA Central Committee, 4th
   Party Congress, 54, 125
Syspeirosi (coiling), 59
Szczerbiak, Aleks, 5, 6

T
Taggart, Paul, 5, 6
Talat, Mehmet Ali, 111
Tassis, Chrysanthos, 32, 48, 49, 94
Teixeira, Nuno, 30
Teperoglou, Eftichia, 46, 94–5, 119
Thatcher, Mark, 14, 118
Theodossopoulos, Dimitrios, 99
Thessaloniki Manifesto, 121
Third way, 14, 30, 34

CPI Antony Rowe
Chippenham, UK
2018-10-11 10:39